0071431

Learning Resources Center
Collin County Community College District
SPRING CREEK CAMPUS
Plano, Texas   75074

FROM *CAN-DO* TO *VOODOO*, A WICKEDLY WISE COLLECTION OF THE WORDS THAT WIN ELECTIONS…OR PULL THE WOOL OVER UN-SAVVY EYES

"In the beginning is the word," and it can win or lose an election. When Dan Quayle warns that the *long knives* are out against Clarence Thomas…when Arkansas Governor Bill Clinton wants to go "beyond the *stale orthodoxies* of the left and right"…when Senator Harris Wofford speechifies, "I'm the kind of Democrat who's against racial discrimination and against racial *quotas*," we realize political language is a minefield of nuances and hidden agendas. Those who don't know the shades of meaning are never going to end up *inside the Beltway*. But this candid, nonpartisan, wryly correct reference work provides *a window of opportunity* for those in the race and a delightful armchair guide for the ever-fascinated spectators of America's truly great pastime…politics.

The Knack of the Political Hack

FREEDOM FIGHTERS—Any favored insurgent army, no matter how cruel its actions or despotic its orientation.

GREATNESS—Always the destiny of the United States. Anyone inclined to argue the point is not destined for electoral greatness.

MELTING POT—An oratorical recipe for America, without mentioning that those at the bottom are most likely to get burned.

RHETORIC, EMPTY—Rhetoric presumably inferior to the full-blown variety.

VOCAL MINORITY—People who are too loud for their numbers, and presumably wrong to boot.

THE POWER OF BABBLE

THE POLITICIAN'S DICTIONARY
OF BUZZWORDS & DOUBLETALK
FOR EVERY OCCASION

THE POWER
OF
BABBLE

THE POLITICIAN'S DICTIONARY
OF BUZZWORDS & DOUBLETALK
FOR EVERY OCCASION

NORMAN SOLOMON

A LAUREL BOOK
Published by
Dell Publishing
a division of
Bantam Doubleday Dell Publishing Group, Inc.
666 Fifth Avenue
New York, New York 10103

If you purchased this book without a cover you should be aware that this book is stolen property. It was reported as "unsold and destroyed" to the publisher and neither the author nor the publisher has received any payment for this "stripped book."

Copyright © 1992 by Norman Solomon

All rights reserved. No part of this book may be reproduced or transmitted in any form or by any means, electronic or mechanical, including photocopying, recording, or by any information storage and retrieval system, without the written permission of the Publisher, except where permitted by law.

The trademark Laurel® is registered in the U.S. Patent and Trademark Office.

The trademark Dell® is registered in the U.S. Patent and Trademark Office.

ISBN: 0-440-21241-3

Printed in the United States of America

Published simultaneously in Canada

July 1992

10 9 8 7 6 5 4 3 2 1

OPM

Introduction

Sure, you'll need pollsters and fund-raisers, ad writers and strategists. But if you want to win the next election, you've got to keep talking—and that's where *The Power of Babble* comes in.

Ambiguity that sounds forthright is a politician's best rhetorical friend. Strive to present your expedient choices as acts of courage; when you stoke the lowest common prejudices, do so with visionary hot air. Keep flattering voters. Don't let on that you're unlikely to lose an election by underestimating their discernment.

Your ultimate weaponry comes down to words. Select only the loaded ones. Take aim with steady determination. Make every verbal bullet count. Learn to fire with a single fluid motion of your tongue, which should always be polished and well oiled.

The Power of Babble will provide you with plenty of ammunition, from the tarmac to the podium. Remember that the best buzzwords commonly precede, and preempt, thought. Used correctly, they can guard against meaning— the most dangerous hazard of political language. Meaning causes big problems. And it's so unnecessary!

Don't shy away from timeworn doubletalk, any more than you would avoid putting bullets in a gun because others just like them have been used before. It's true that the wrong cliché, ill chosen and poorly aimed, can shoot you in the foot. But the right one will find its mark: the voter.

Of course, you should not acknowledge that you've ever seen this book. Keep it out of view of snooping reporters. (These days, that means off any bookshelves visible from windows.) If pressed to comment on *The Power of Babble,* insist that you have never picked it up, but you understand that it is despicably cynical, you believe in the integrity of words, the sanctity of the public trust, etc.

Thousands of effective speeches and deft press releases can result from proper use of *The Power of Babble.* Here's an example of a combative statement—chock full of potential sound-bites. With the help of this book, it's as easy as A-B-C.

"America bashing and anti-Western appeasement may appeal to atheists, but such backroom bankruptcy is barbaric bean counting inside the Beltway, where Big Brother is big government with a blank check. Boys on the bus don't seem to mind the breakdown of the family. With the brie-and-white-wine set and their burdensome budgets, a bureaucracy of cheap-shot class conflict is fueling costly cradle-to-grave criminality. The demagoguery is divisive. Doom-and-gloom feds promote a feeding frenzy—aided by flimflammers, flip-flops, herd journalists, ideologues, and influence peddlers. Impotent insiders are in sync with instability, intolerance, irresponsible labor bosses, loopholes, and mudslinging. This great nation has grown overdependent on PACs, partisanship, personal attacks, perversion, and pessimists. The people must not be polarized as political footballs for pork-barreling, power-hungry profligates and their propaganda. What's more, we have no need for protectionist pundits. Quotas—with the reckless red tape of reverse discrimination and the rhetoric of self-appointed, self-styled sixties radicals—bring sleepless nights, sloganeering, and smears. With smoke and mirrors and smoke-filled rooms, soak-the-rich spendthrifts are strident as they tax and spend. These threats are tragic, tyrannical, unethical, and even unpatriotic—the work of vested interests, the Vietnam syndrome, violence, waste, welfare, wheeler-dealers, and wrangling zealots."

See—it's easy!

Of course, you'll want to exude plenty of positive, reassuring messages, too. Here's a sample, again alphabetized for easy reference:

"America is back, and bipartisan—biting the bullet with competitiveness, diplomacy, efficiency, empowerment, end games, and environmentalism, along with faith in the Founding Fathers, freedom's blessings, free markets and free peoples, and most of all, God. Our great heritage has held the line for human rights, individual initiative, justice, kids, leadership, liberty, loyalty, mainstream values, the marketplace, measured responses, melting pots, the middle class, military reform, moderates, modernization, moral standards, national security, and Old Glory. Opportunity comes from optimism, patriotism, peace through strength, the people, pluralism, and points of light. Pragmatism and the power of prayer make for principle, while the private sector protects the public interest. Realism can mean recycling, self-discipline, and the spirit of '76, bringing stability and standing tall for strategic interests and streamlined taxation. Uncle Sam has been undaunted ever since Valley Forge, with values venerated by veterans: vigilance, vigor, vision, voluntarism, and Western values."

Nothing to it!

May the power of babble be with you.

The use of words ... arouse ideas. Rarely ...
requires not only ... writer should ...
but that they ... be understood ...
exclusively ...
ous as to ... writer ... conveys to ...
or so correct as ... arouses many equivalents ...
different ideas.

This volume is ...

"When I use a word," Humpty Dumpty said, in rather a
scornful tone, "it means just what I choose it to mean—
neither more nor less."

"The question is," said Alice, "whether you can make
words mean so many different things."

"The question is," said Humpty Dumpty, "which is to be
master—that's all."

—Lewis Carroll
Through the Looking-Glass

The use of words is to express ideas. Perspicuity, therefore, requires not only that the ideas should be distinctly formed, but that they should be expressed by words distinctly and exclusively appropriate to them. But no language is so copious as to supply words and phrases for every complex idea, or so correct as not to include many equivocally denoting different ideas.

—JAMES MADISON,
The Federalist (XXXVII)

This volume is born of the reminder that "in the beginning is the word"—and particularly so, in the case of a democratic government. For in such a government it is the freely spoken and freely challenged word that is meant to lay open a vision of the realities lying beyond the sweep of naked eyesight. Surely, then, the first duty of an officer in a democratic government is to uphold the integrity of words used in public debate; and to do this by himself using them in ways where they will stand as one with the things they are meant to represent.

—JOHN F. KENNEDY,
The Strategy of Peace

"When *I* use a word," Humpty Dumpty said, in rather a scornful tone, "it means just what I choose it to mean—neither more nor less."

"The question is," said Alice, "whether you *can* make words mean so many different things."

"The question is," said Humpty Dumpty, "which is to be master—that's all."

—LEWIS CARROLL,
Through the Looking-Glass

Aa Bb

"A" is for American Dream
"B" is for Big Government

aberration
No cause for concern.
USAGE: Insistence that the event or pattern is a fluke.

The impropriety committed by my aide was an unfortunate *aberration*.

Antonym: *case-in-point*

abortion on demand
USAGE: Frequent repetition of this term is appropriate if your public position favors banning abortions. But if you're supporting abortion rights, never use this phrase—it makes females seeking abortions sound so . . . demanding. Since some weighty cultural strictures remain against women demanding much of anything, "abortion on demand" summons up a plethora of negative images about pushy women who don't know their place. By implication, if women are certain they can obtain "abortions on demand," who knows what they'll be demanding next?

"I'd like the [U.S.] Supreme Court to review *Roe v. Wade* —not only review, but change it. I think it's far too liberal. It's led to *abortion on demand.* I don't think that's right." (Representative Jack Kemp, December 19, 1987)

"I am convinced that new medical innovation and new social developments are changing the ground-rules of the abortion debate—shifting the burden of proof to the advocates of *abortion on demand.*" (Senator Dan Coats, September 1989)

across-the-board
An approach that sounds even handed, as though no one should have reason to complain when budgets don't meet needs or when taxation remains unbalanced.

"I personally favor a tax cut. . . . And it must be an *across-the-board* approach—one that will not only put more money in the hands of consumers and purchasers but also will put more money in the hands of investors and job creators." (Richard M. Nixon, March 10, 1958)

activist federal judges
U.S. judges being denounced for their decisions.
USAGE: Take care not to mention that any judge can be called "activist" in response to disputed rulings. For good measure, portray the judges as contemptuous of common folk and eager to take advantage of their constitutional independence.

"Mr. President, the problem in the matter of school prayer, as in so many areas of constitutional law, is that in the last two and a half decades *activist federal judges,* with lifetime appointments and no accountability, elitists posing as egalitarians, have overstepped their bounds under the Constitution and usurped the power of Congress and the states, imposing their own personal views of good public policy on the American public, irrespective of the Constitution." (Senator Jesse Helms, January 14, 1991)

adrift
So a new captain must be needed at the helm to steer the ship of state.

"We have been a nation *adrift* too long." (Jimmy Carter, July 15, 1976)

"America is *adrift* as our leaders flinch from the difficult decisions that will safeguard us from the energy and environmental threats that confront us." (former senator Paul E. Tsongas, March 1991)

See also: *buck stops here, the*

advisory
Without power but potentially impressive.

USAGE: Enables issues to be referred to others, whose advice can later be embraced or ignored, as convenient.

"We have come a long way since the *Exxon Valdez* ran aground on Bligh Reef. New measures have been established to greatly minimize the risks that could lead to oil spills. . . . [A] citizen *advisory* committee has been established for oversight of terminal and tanker operations." (Senator Frank H. Murkowski, August 2, 1991)

See also: *nonbinding*

affluent society
USAGE: A phrase that summons up images of well-being and contentment; implies that those who don't share in the affluence are out of step, insignificant, or at fault.

"The United States has become an *affluent society*. . . ." (Representative Eligio de la Garza, October 19, 1990)

See also: *economic expansion*

afraid to walk the streets
Terrified of violent crime.

USAGE: Conveying that you understand deep worries about criminal elements, this phrase can lay rhetorical groundwork for chipping away at interpretations of the Bill of Rights that you don't like.

"It is no wonder that our wives and daughters are *afraid to walk the streets* at night out of fear that they will be the next statistic." (Senator Strom Thurmond, March 13, 1991, speaking in support of the Comprehensive Violent Crime Control Act.)

See also: *crime; law and order; rapists*

aggression
Any military attack that one does not launch or favor.
USAGE: All you want to do is prevent it or stop it.
"Our purpose is solely to defend against *aggression*." (Lyndon B. Johnson, February 23, 1966)
"Our patience and our perseverance will match our power. *Aggression* will never prevail." (Lyndon B. Johnson, January 17, 1968)

See also: *naked aggression*

air quality
Extent of ability to breathe without interference from pollution.
USAGE: Encourages people to think in terms of the oxygen still in the air rather than the oxygen their lungs are being deprived of.
"Because of the proximity of these public lands to our population centers and transportation corridors, expansion of our industrial base may present problems under the Clean Air Act even though it would not cause any significant deterioration in *air quality*." (Senator Frank H. Murkowski, July 18, 1991)

See also: *clean air*

aliens
Noncitizens living in the United States.
USAGE: Choice of this word can evoke vague feelings that

Americans must protect what's theirs against encroachment close to home.

Antonym: *immigrants*

aliens, illegal
People who have entered and/or remained inside U.S. borders in violation of the law.

USAGE: Implies that the United States is under siege from within.

"It's not just a sieve; it's a gaping hole in law enforcement today. Individuals who are not supposed to be employed in this country are able to be employed through the use of illegal documents. And if we don't stop the use of illegal documents, we're not going to stop the employment of *illegal aliens*." (Representative Lamar Smith, June 23, 1991)

Antonym: many of our ancestors who came to these shores

all Americans
A sweeping hyperbole, false literally but effective rhetorically.

"This is truly a great victory for all of us—*all Americans,* all allies, and particularly the people of Kuwait." (Representative Jim Ramstad, March 5, 1991)

See also: *American people, the; people, the*

all men are created equal
USAGE: One of those phrases so venerated and timeworn that no one would expect any particular conclusion to follow as to policy.

"Let us discard all this quibbling about this man and the other man, this race and that race and the other race being inferior, and therefore they must be placed in an inferior position. Let us discard all these things, and unite as one people throughout this land, until we shall once more stand up declaring that *all men are created equal.*" (Abraham Lincoln, July 1858, campaigning for the U.S. Senate in Chicago.) Compare with Lincoln's statement campaigning in the southern Illinois town of Charleston two months later: "I will say, then, that I am not, nor ever have been, in favor of bringing about in any way the social and political equality of the white and black races; that I am not, nor ever have been, in favor of making voters or jurors of negroes, nor of qualifying them to hold office, nor to intermarry with white people. . . . And inasmuch as they cannot so live, while they do remain together there must be the position of superior and inferior, and I as much as any other man am in favor of having the superior position assigned to the white race."

Derivation: Declaration of Independence, July 4, 1776. ("We hold these Truths to be self-evident, that all Men are created equal, that they are endowed by their Creator with certain unalienable Rights, that among these are Life, Liberty, and the Pursuit of Happiness. . . .")

ambiguity
Blurring of right and wrong.
USAGE: Especially helpful in responding to accusations that you violated campaign-finance regulations.

America, God bless the United States of
Simultaneous exclamation of fervent piety and patriotism.
USAGE: An indisputable and unsurpassed way of closing important speeches. Has a ring of devout authority.

"And so, good-bye, God bless you, and *God bless the United States of America.*" (Ronald Reagan, January 11, 1989)

"God bless you and *God bless the United States of America.*" (George Bush, January 20, 1989)

See also: *blessed land; God bless you; under God*

America, the promise of

USAGE: America, of course, has always been big on promises; no reason to stop now. To maximize impact, you may want to weave into a sentimental story about a parent, grandparent, etc.

"*The promise of America* is a simple promise: Every person shall share in the blessings of this land. And they shall share on the basis of their merits as a person." (Lyndon B. Johnson, March 13, 1965)

". . . arrived at Ellis Island with only $25 in his pocket, but with a deep and abiding faith in *the promise of America.*" (Michael Dukakis, July 21, 1988)

America bashing

To patriotism what sacrilege is to religiosity.

"If they are going to call us Japan bashers, let us tell it like it is: This is stone-cold *America bashing.* I think we should stand up for No. 1, America." (Representative James A. Traficant, Jr., July 11, 1991)

See also: *number one*

America is back

National strength and resurgence.

USAGE: Especially suitable after recent election to higher office.

See also: *renewal*

America means business

Uncle Sam stars as The Terminator.

"One of the objectives of the war in the Gulf was to show

tyrants who might imitate Saddam Hussein that they can't invade, rape and pillage their neighbors and hope to get away with it. A speedy and thorough war crimes trial will show the world that *America means business.*" (Representative William S. Broomfield, May 21, 1991)

See also: *war criminals*

American century, the next
A phrase for evoking national grandeur yet to come.

"This is not merely a call for new government initiatives, it is a call for new initiative in government, in our communities, and from every American—to prepare for *the next American century.* . . . We will get on our way to a new record of expansion and achieve the competitive strength that will carry us into *the next American century.*" (George Bush, January 29, 1991)

"Under Ronald Reagan's guiding hand, the premature reports of America's decline gave way to pride and conviction for *the next American century.*" (Senator Frank H. Murkowski, February 6, 1991)

Antonym: *decline*
See also: *superpower, only*

American dream, the
Aggregate upbeat hopes of Americans. An aged cliché that has remained aloft in the annals of high-flung rhetoric.
USAGE: Can resonate with upscale college-educated and lower-income strata alike.

"All of us want our children to have a better life than we had, and it should be the constant aim of each generation to make things better for the next. It has always been a part of *the American dream,* and I think we have been successful in accomplishing it to a most remarkable degree." (Harry S Truman, May 12, 1950)

"Dishonest political promises to selfish groups—not rebuffed at the ballot box—can make a nightmare of *the American dream*. But wise and determined performance of our civic duties can make that dream come true." (Dwight D. Eisenhower, October 25, 1949)

"Our own freedom and growth have never been the final goal of *the American dream*. We were never meant to be an oasis of liberty and abundance in a worldwide desert of disappointed dreams." (Lyndon B. Johnson, January 4, 1965)

"*The American dream* does not come to those who fall asleep." (Richard M. Nixon, January 20, 1969)

"*The American dream* endures." (Jimmy Carter, January 20, 1977)

"We've polished up *the American dream*." (Ronald Reagan, July 8, 1987)

"That's what this election is really all about. It's about *the American dream*—those who want to keep it for the few, and those who know it must be nurtured and passed along." (Texas State treasurer Ann W. Richards, July 18, 1988)

"We're going to win because we are the party that believes in *the American dream*, a dream so powerful that . . ." (Michael Dukakis, July 21, 1988)

"Michael Dukakis talks . . . about putting *the American dream* back in the reach of all the American people. . . . My father is a symbol of what people of courage and vision and daring can achieve in America. He has lived *the American dream*, the dream we want to come true for our children. . . . Now that's *the American dream* that we have nourished and protected for two hundred years—the dream of freedom and opportunity, the chance for a step up in life." (Senator Lloyd M. Bentsen, July 21, 1988)

"If these conditions continue, can we preserve America's leadership in the world we've done so much to make? Can we keep *the American dream* alive here at home?" (Arkansas governor Bill Clinton, May 6, 1991)

"As leaders of our nation it is time to realize that we can no longer afford to overlook the impact of legislation on small businesses. It is imperative that we look after the champions of *the American dream.*" (Representative Wayne Allard, May 1991)

"I don't have anything against the wealthy. Striking it rich is *the American dream.*" (Representative Dave Obey, May 10, 1991)

"Thousands of whole and good communities already flourish in America—communities where ordinary people have achieved *the American dream.*" (George Bush, June 12, 1991)

American family, the
A certain kind of family in the United States. Of course, many different family arrangements exist—including millions of single parents, unmarried lovers, collective households, and gay or lesbian couples. While commonly leaving such social relationships unacknowledged, politicians keep idealizing "the American family" suitable for Norman Rockwell portraits—in effect wishing away many de facto families, rendered virtually invisible in political discussions. USAGE: Pushes buttons ranging from memories of *Father Knows Best* to yearnings for predivorce family relationships.

"And I join in the hope that when my time as your President has ended, people might say this about our Nation . . . that we had strengthened *the American family,* which is the basis of our society." (Jimmy Carter, January 20, 1977)

"And we didn't set a weathervane on top of the Golden Gate Bridge before we started talking about *the American family.*" (Ronald Reagan, August 1984)

"It's time to wake up with new challenges that face *the American family. . . .*" (Michael Dukakis, July 21, 1988)

See also: *family; pro-family; values, family*

American life

Implicitly or explicitly, the most important and valuable human life.

USAGE: A good phrase for ratcheting up the emotional pitch.

"Ollie North . . . believed passionately in something. He believed passionately that every *American life* is precious. . . . And one of the things I feel deeply is that when *American life* is threatened, or when an American man or woman is held against his or her will, we've got to care about that." (George Bush, December 5, 1987)

"None of us wants to see *American lives* lost. . . . A settlement now, however, that allows Iraq to retain its tools of military and economic aggression will precipitate a bloody, protracted, and possibly unwinnable war in the future. . . . I am honored and humbled to be here, and will do my utmost to protect *American lives* and work for a durable peace." (Senator John Seymour, January 12, 1991)

American people, the

A catchall way to generalize about the attitudes, interests, and qualities of an entire population.

USAGE: They should be depicted as good-spirited, perceptive, and blameless.

"A national effort, entailing sacrifices by *the American people,* is now under way to make long-overdue improvements in our military posture. *The American people* support this effort because they understand how fundamental it is to keeping the peace they so fervently desire." (Ronald Reagan, June 9, 1982)

SPRING CREEK CAMPUS WITHDRAWN

"I think I understand all *the American people.*" (Senator Robert Dole, January 2, 1988)

"I intend to do everything I can to see that the AIDS immigration prohibition remains in place. If I lose, *the American people* will lose also." (Senator Jesse Helms, January 14, 1991)

"Throughout Operation Desert Storm, *the American people* stood behind our Armed Forces without regard to partisan politics." (Representative Dante Fascell, March 5, 1991)

"There's nothing wrong with *the American people.*" (Arkansas governor Bill Clinton, June 15, 1991)

See also: *all Americans; people, the*

American people, the genius of the

A fawning bit of political phraseology based on the assumption that flattery may get you somewhere.

"Today, we see an American economic renaissance. Tax cuts, deregulation, and low inflation have freed *the* entrepreneurial *genius of the American people.* . . ." (Ronald Reagan, February 6, 1986)

"A political party can do well at the local level only if it reflects *the genius of the American people.*" (Georgia Democratic Party chair John Henry Anderson, July 18, 1988)

"Mr. Speaker, it was seven years ago this week when Ronald Reagan in a speech from the White House mobilized *the genius of the American people* and challenged our brightest minds to build a defensive system that would protect us from nuclear attack." (Representative Dana Rohrabacher, March 21, 1990)

SPRING WITHDRAWN

American way, the
A diffuse and glowing gloss for America, which has so many "ways" that this phrase functions as a nationalistic Rorschach test.
USAGE: As you please.

"I just don't think it's *the American way* to bring a good man down by rumor and insinuation." (George Bush, July 12, 1991, speaking of his nominee to head the CIA, Robert Gates.)

"How are you going to get ahead in the world? By hard work—that was always *the American way*. But now, no longer do our people . . ." (Dwight D. Eisenhower, November 1966)

Fulbright Fellowship students made statements "condemning *the American way* of life and praising the Communist form of government." (Senator Joseph R. McCarthy, July 24, 1953)

America's peace
USAGE: A means of equating peace on American terms—and national tranquillity—with true peace elsewhere in the world.

"Let us all understand that the question before us is not whether some Americans are for peace and some Americans are against peace. The question at issue is not whether Johnson's war becomes Nixon's war. The great question is: How can we win *America's peace*?" (Richard M. Nixon, November 3, 1969)

anguish
Humility, sincerity, deep feeling.
USAGE: For efforts to deflect anger; can help to mollify public ire.

"For seven and a half years I have worked with a great

President. . . . And I've seen modest decisions made with *anguish,* and crucial decisions made with dispatch." (George Bush, August 18, 1988)

"During the Persian Gulf war, nine British soldiers were killed as a result of 'friendly fire' from an American air-craft. . . . We want our British friends to know that we share their *anguish* and we share their grief." (Representative Tom Lantos, July 25, 1991)

Antonym: arrogance
See also: *sleepless nights*

answering the call
Implies a duty so automatic that thinking about it should be unnecessary, as in the case of going to war.

"*Answering the call* made others free." (George Bush, June 8, 1991)

anti-American
Reprehensible, threatening, envious from afar.

anti-Christian
Human activities that do not fit within the speaker's definition of "Christian."
USAGE: Plays well to most fundamentalist galleries.

"Advocating condom use has accomplished one thing, Mr. President. It has put this Government's stamp of approval on the *anti-Christian* ideals of the sexual revolution, a revolution that can be credited with family breakups, rising abortions, rising out-of-wedlock births, rising VD rates, and rising school dropout rates." (Senator Jesse Helms, January 14, 1991)

"While some are using the AIDS issue to promote political and societal acceptance of an *anti-Christian* lifestyle, thousands of innocent Americans are dying." (Senator Jesse Helms, January 14, 1991)

See also: *innocent Americans; values, Christian*

anti-trust
Rare.

Legal actions against corporations for becoming too large and monopolistic. So out of favor has "anti-trust" become among politicians who have earned corporate trust that when the term is used, it's likely to be part of a complaint that government regulations are too stringent.

"Current *anti-trust* laws prevent American companies from joint venturing in almost any area, including such critical ones as research and development. . . . American companies should be released from *anti-trust* constraints in areas which impact on their capabilities in international trade." (former senator Paul E. Tsongas, March 1991)

anti-Western
Hostile to the goals of the United States and its closest allies.
USAGE: Similar to "anti-American" but broader.

"Even after we win on the battlefield, and we will win, there is a grave danger that the latent anti-imperialistic, fundamentalist, and *anti-Western* hostility that exists will explode to the detriment of American interests for decades to come." (Senator Joseph R. Biden, Jr., January 24, 1991)

appearance of improprieties
Just looks bad, but presumably isn't.

"Clearly, no one regrets more than I do the *appearance of improprieties* produced as a result of the events surrounding my recent travel." (White House chief of staff John H. Sununu, June 22, 1991)

See also: *improprieties*

appearance problem
Just looks bad, but presumably isn't.

John Sununu's travel created "an *appearance problem.*" (George Bush, June 19, 1991)

appeasement
A righteous description of any action or inaction deemed overly accommodating to a bad-guy government.
USAGE: Implies similarity to British prime minister Neville Chamberlain's capitulation to Adolf Hitler at the Munich conference just prior to World War II. Almost guaranteed to send many liberals running for cover.

"If the history of the 1930s teaches us anything, it is that *appeasement* of dictators is the sure road to world war. If aggression were allowed to succeed in Korea, it would be an open invitation to new acts of aggression elsewhere." (Harry S Truman, September 1, 1950)

"America is allergic to *appeasement.* There will be no appeasing Communist aggression while I am President." (Dwight D. Eisenhower, October 20, 1958)

"While we must never answer insults in kind, we must leave no doubt at any time that in Berlin or in Cuba or anywhere else in the world, America will not tolerate being pushed around by anybody. We have already paid a terrible price in lives and resources to learn that *appeasement* leads not to peace but to war." (Richard M. Nixon, July 28, 1960)

"The American people want to be a part of no war. But the American people want no part of *appeasement* or of any aggression." (Lyndon B. Johnson, June 3, 1965)

"Together, we have resisted the trap of *appeasement,* cyn-

icism, and isolation that gives temptation to tyrants."
(George Bush, January 29, 1991)

"They're not for peace. They're for *appeasement*. . . .
They ought to go to the Iraqi Embassy and demonstrate for
peace." (Senator Phil Gramm, February 1991, referring to
antiwar protesters outside the White House.)

Antonym: *pragmatism*

armed vigilance
Readiness for military intervention.
USAGE: Makes the flexing of military prowess sound noble,
wise, and defensive.

Synonym: *military preparedness*

arms control
A way of managing the armaments race between the
world's major powers.
USAGE: These days almost everyone is for "arms control"
because the term doesn't mean much per se. Thus it can be
a useful phrase to woo voters who want the United States
to build as many nuclear weapons as possible, as well as
voters who favor disarmament.

"It is not inconsistent to say, on the one hand, we're
interested in *arms control* and, on the other hand, we want
to make certain our friends can defend themselves." (Secretary of Defense Dick Cheney, June 4, 1991)

See also: *modernization; nuclear stockpile, total*

assault from foreign competition
Vigorous trade depicted as an attack on national sovereignty.

"North Carolina furniture and textile companies . . .
are already under *assault from foreign competition*." (Senator Jesse Helms, January 14, 1991)

assurance

A promise that may not be kept.

USAGE: Convenient for calming fears.

"And while I am talking to you mothers and fathers, I give you one more *assurance*. I have said this before, but I shall say it again and again and again: Your boys are not going to be sent into any foreign wars." (Franklin D. Roosevelt, October 30, 1940, campaign speech in Boston)

atheists

USAGE: Can be helpful in such tasks as disparaging those who oppose prayer in public school.

"I don't know that *atheists* should be considered as citizens, nor should they be considered patriots. This is one nation under God." (George Bush, August 27, 1987)

"What I was saying is that those people, especially in the ACLU, many of whom are *atheists,* have done everything they can to use the Constitution to take away the religious life in our community which indeed is the only guarantee that we will have liberty. George Washington said the same thing." (Pat Robertson, February 13, 1988)

Antonym: *God-fearing*

See also: *prayer in schools; under God*

attrit

A new verb (root of "attrition") for killing.

USAGE: Bloodless euphemism. Can make even the most horrific massacre sound abstract.

Our forces will *attrit* the enemy as needed.

Derivation: U.S. Army Lt. Gen. Thomas Kelly, at Pentagon press briefings in early 1991, describing war with Iraq.

See also: *surgical strikes*

austerity measures
Code words for economic steps detrimental to the well-being of large numbers of people.

In the long run, these *austerity measures* will benefit the entire society.

See also: *bite the bullet; debt crisis*

autonomy
In foreign affairs, commonly a faint sound of self-determination to go along with the substance of subjugation.
USAGE: When an ethnic or national group is undergoing occupation or annexation, you can urge "autonomy" to imply sympathy for their predicament when you don't want to support their self-rule.

"Camp David envisioned *autonomy* for the Palestinians in the West Bank and Gaza. It did not—I repeat, I am talking about the Camp David accord—it did not provide for the creation of a Palestinian state, no matter what the pro-Arab factions in the U.S. Department of State would now have us believe." (Senator Jesse Helms, July 26, 1991)

See also: *self-determination*

awe
Suitable reverence.

"There is a sense of *awe* at how brilliantly Bush has handled this." (Representative Newt Gingrich, August 1991)

back room
Sneaky; behind the scenes; not aboveboard.

Unlike my opponent, I don't make *back room* deals.

See also: *smoke-filled rooms*

bad press
Negative publicity.
USAGE: Can imply that spurious reasons or questionable motives account for being singled out for critical news coverage.

"Indeed, it appears as though the Sound is well on its way to recovery. Exxon, on the other hand, continues to suffer from *bad press*." (Representative Philip M. Crane, September 11, 1990)

bailout
Rescue of failing private institutions via massive financial subsidies from the U.S. Treasury.
USAGE: Often conveys necessity, summoning images of bailing out a boat in danger of sinking. Comparisons to household budgeting can be helpful, however irrelevant.

Antonym: *giveaway at taxpayers' expense*

balance of power
A configuration of geopolitical leverage (regional or global) that the speaker finds satisfactory.

We must act to maintain the present *balance of power* in that part of the world.

Antonym: *instability*
See also: *stability*

balance of powers
In national politics, the invoked principle of three coequal branches of government.
USAGE: To make a case that the executive or legislative or judicial branch has become overly powerful, that branch can be charged with disrupting the proper balance.

The *balance of powers* enshrined in our Constitution is in jeopardy.

Synonym: *separation of powers*
See also: *enshrined*

balanced budget

USAGE: A holy grail of politics, *balanced budget* is to be sought after if never found. It moves like a horizon on a long journey, never near but never out of sight.

"A *balanced budget* is an essential first measure in checking further depreciation in the buying power of the dollar." (Dwight D. Eisenhower, February 2, 1953)

"And what we need is a constitutional amendment that requires a *balanced budget*." (Ronald Reagan, November 28, 1987)

balls

Testicular metaphor for vigorous courage.

USAGE: Obviously not appropriate for female candidates.

"Who says I don't have *balls*?" (Edmund S. Muskie, March 1972, to reporters, shooting baskets on a playground in Stickney, Illinois.)

Caution: Acceptable only in certain settings; the advantages, such as male bonding with male journalists and demonstrated earthiness to counteract image problems in other directions, must be assessed as trade-offs against giving offense or being perceived as crude or vulgar.

See also: *kick ass; stick*

bankrupt policies

Failed political programs of opponents.

USAGE: An epithet that can be applied to the records of most incumbents.

In place of the *bankrupt policies* of the past, I offer . . .

barbarian
USAGE: These days an epithet customarily reserved for selected foreigners.

Andrew Jackson is a *"barbarian* who could hardly spell
his own name." (John Quincy Adams, 1829)

barbarism
Often, in time of war, the more that the United States has
engaged in slaughter of civilians, the more U.S. politicians
have denounced the "barbarism" of the other side.
USAGE: To describe actions that are as depraved and cruel
as ours are virtuous and kind.

"Regardless of one's opinion of the war, or of the bombings of North Vietnam, there is no justification and no excuse for the personal reprisals now threatened by Hanoi
against individual American pilots. . . . I have dissented
at many points from this war and its conduct. But I am at
one with all Americans in regarding any reprisals against
these young men and indirectly against their families, as an
intolerable act—contrary to the laws of war, contrary to all
past practices in this war, a plunge into *barbarism* which
could serve the interest of no man and no nation." (Robert
F. Kennedy, July 15, 1966)

See also: *terrorism*

barring God from our classrooms
Enforcing separation between organized religion and the
state, as stipulated by the 1962 U.S. Supreme Court ruling
that forbade prayer in public schools.
USAGE: Summons images of the Lord being sent home from
school—a sacrilege perpetrated by the secular. Most suitable for fundamentalist constituencies.

"Mr. President, *barring God from our classrooms* was not

the intent of our Founding Fathers who wrote the U.S. Constitution." (Senator Jesse Helms, January 14, 1991)

See also: *intolerance of Christianity*

beacon of hope
Almost invariably a reference to the United States.
USAGE: This phrase flatters the American proclivity to see the United States as the inspirational center of the globe.

"Let us pledge together to make these next four years the best four years in America's history, so that on its 200th birthday America will be as young and as vital as when it began, and as bright a *beacon of hope* for all the world." (Richard M. Nixon, January 20, 1973)

"Help us to win support for those who struggle for the same freedoms we hold dear. In doing so, we will not just be helping them, we will be helping ourselves, our children, and all the peoples of the world. We'll be demonstrating that America is still a *beacon of hope,* still a light unto the nations." (Ronald Reagan, February 2, 1988)

"If we don't stand for the correct path to the future no one else will. And that correct path is democracy, capitalism, and individual liberty. We are the *beacon of hope* for the whole world. We owe it to the world as well as ourselves to understand that critical fact clearly." (Senator Albert Gore, Jr., April 12, 1991)

bean counting
Undue attention to minute detail; fixation on numerical trivia.

Like some modern-day Nero, my opponent has been *bean counting* while society burns.

The many serious problems besetting our city/county/state/nation require leaders, not *bean counters.*

Antonyms: cold hard facts; *realism*
See also: *forest for the trees*

beasts

USAGE: Treading lightly, you may be able to pull off comparing foreign adversaries to "beasts" without seeming heavy-handed.

"[A]ncient man survived the more powerful *beasts* about him because his wisdom—his strategy and his policies—overcame his lack of power. We can do the same." (John F. Kennedy, August 14, 1958)

bedrock

Paved surface that serves as a runway for many a rhetorical takeoff. ("Nation" or "country" can often be found in nearby airspace.)

"The ideal of equal opportunity, I believe, is the *bedrock* ideal of our society and of our system." (Lyndon B. Johnson, July 7, 1964)

"Families are the *bedrock* of our nation—teachers of cooperation, tolerance, concern, and responsibility." (Ronald Reagan, February 9, 1982)

"We believe that America is a country where small business owners must succeed, because they are the *bedrock*, backbone of our economy." (Texas State treasurer Ann W. Richards, July 18, 1988)

"The Democrats think that people make politics in the 21st century. People. People are not little items in some economic game. People are the *bedrock* on which our country will rise or fall." (Arkansas governor Bill Clinton, June 15, 1991)

behavior
USAGE: By focusing on "behavior" of people needing assistance from government programs, it is easy to imply that they have been taking advantage of federal, state, and local agencies.

"The National Commission on AIDS says that the disease deserves more funding because it is contagious while diabetes, cancer, and heart disease are not. In fact, AIDS is contagious through *behavior.* A change in *behavior* among two high risk populations, homosexual men and IV drug users, would reduce the spread of this disease without one more dime of Federal money or the discovery of a cure." (Senator Jesse Helms, January 14, 1991)

"If we are going to be the party of government . . . we can't have people think we are captives of our own bureaucracy and that we don't recognize any responsibility on the part of the people who benefit from government programs to give something back in terms of responsible *behavior.*" (Arkansas governor Bill Clinton, June 1991)

See also: *privilege; responsibility*

below the belt
The location of a low—or telling—blow.

". . . the entire issue reminded voters of Nixon and Watergate. Earlier, seizing eagerly upon all these matters, Carter had struck *below the belt.*" (Gerald R. Ford, 1979)

"Harry Truman 'gave 'em hell'—but he never hit *below the belt.* It would have been totally out of character—and he didn't need to, anyway." (Hubert H. Humphrey, September 14, 1964)

Antonym: *rough-and-tumble*
See also: *cheap shot*

Beltway, inside the

Washington, D.C.

A pejorative usually aimed at congressional incumbents and their supporters in Washington. The innuendos include elitism, distance, insularity, and untoward hunger for power.

USAGE: Don't hesitate to denounce people "inside the Beltway" just because you are inside the Beltway yourself; it's done all the time, and merely reflects the fact that your best political rhetoric is apt to be symbolic (and simplistic) rather than literal (or realistic).

"Mr. Chairman, I rise in strong support of the efforts by my colleague, the gentleman from California, to offer an alternative to the *inside-the-Beltway* groupthink that now dominates our budget deliberations." (Representative C. Christopher Cox, April 17, 1991)

"I'll be darned if I'm going to knuckle in to a handful of people *inside the Beltway* who say, 'Jump,' and then the Democratic senators say, 'How high?' " (George Bush, June 1991, speaking about civil rights legislation at a Republican fundraising event.)

See also: *under an air conditioner*

Beltway, outside the

Mental regions with a prevalence of logic and reason, real or imagined. Presumably the opposite of "inside the Beltway."

". . . *outside the Beltway* this [Tsongas campaign] message resonates." (former senator Paul E. Tsongas, July 1991)

See also: *common sense*

benign neglect
Usually a purposeful refusal to help.
USAGE: With rare exceptions, too cryptic, self-contradictory, and candid for public advocacy.
Modern derivation: Memo from Daniel Patrick Moynihan to President-elect Richard Nixon, written prior to Nixon's January 1969 inauguration and leaked in early 1970, in which Moynihan wrote that "the time may have come when the issue of race could benefit from a period of benign neglect." He argued for "trying to create some equivalence between what Government can do about certain problems and how much attention it draws to them."
See also: *big government; paternalism; welfare*

best interests of the country
A ready-made rationale for any and all actions.
"In 1986, I was faced with some very difficult decisions. I did what I thought was in the *best interests of the country*. Today, I was faced with equally difficult decisions. I have done what I think is in the *best interests of the country* and what the Constitution requires of me." (former CIA official Alan D. Fiers, Jr., July 10, 1991, admitting that he lied to Congress in 1986 about CIA knowledge of the diversion of Iran arms-sales profits to the contras.)

big business
An ominous-sounding moniker that casts large corporations in a bad light.
Caution: Use of this term, while perhaps suitable for campaigners who rely on small, individual donations, is hazardous if depending on corporate contributions.

big government

A pejorative for some federal, state, and local agencies.

USAGE: Customarily selective, this phrase refers to agencies regulating corporate activities, or social service programs aiding poor and moderate-income people. It is rarely applied to military or police institutions.

"You can also count on me to continue fighting government waste, higher taxes, and the growth of *big government*." (Representative Mel Hancock, December 1990)

"The best view of *big government* is in the rearview mirror as you're driving away from it." (Ronald Reagan, March 24, 1982)

See also: *bureaucracy; paternalism; red tape*

bigwigs

A put-down of people with wealth and power.

USAGE: Excellent for playing to the populist gallery.

The *bigwigs* may not understand, but . . .

bipartisan

Backed by both major political parties; above partisan motives or advantage.

USAGE: Suggests altruism, overarching concern with the greater good rather than narrow political gain. Often involved is the calculated judgment that both parties must present themselves to be on the same bandwagon with equal fervor.

"We're asking you to come walk with us down the new path of hope and opportunity, and we'll make it a *bipartisan* salvation of our country." (Ronald Reagan, October 26, 1984)

Synonym: *country above party*

Antonym: *partisan*

bipartisanship
A staccato concept, to be invoked and revoked as convenient.
"A new breeze is blowing, and the old *bipartisanship* must be made new again." (George Bush, January 20, 1989)
Antonyms: *partisan bickering; public squabbling*

birthright
Prerogatives and freedoms that should be guaranteed to all.
USAGE: A lofty way for you to encourage voters to feel cheated if they haven't been getting what they deserve.
"Democrats agree that decent housing, a clean environment, a good education and quality health care should be the *birthright* of every American citizen and not the private domain of a privileged few." (Senator Lloyd M. Bentsen, July 21, 1988)

bite the bullet
In economic policy, primarily the making of difficult belt-tightening choices that anger some; more generally, deciding to make tough decisions.
USAGE: Connotations include being in charge with leadership that is manly, masterful, courageous, unafraid of adversity or the slings and arrows of misfortune.
Far too many politicians are unwilling to *bite the bullet.* I am not among them.
See also: *austerity measures*

blame-America-first crowd
USAGE: When you're sick and tired of noisy criticisms aimed at government policies, stir this phrase into a cauldron of vilification.
"What we cannot be proud of, Mr. Speaker, is the un-

shaven, shaggy-haired, drug culture, poor excuses for Americans, wearing their tiny, round wire-rim glasses, a protester's symbol of the *blame-America-first crowd,* out in front of the White House burning the American flag." (Representative Gerald B. H. Solomon, January 17, 1991)

See also: *poor excuses for Americans*

blank check
See: *giveaway at taxpayers' expense*

bleeding heart
A contemptuous term for supporters of policies deemed excessively humanitarian.

USAGE: May be more serviceable for defense than attack. In certain precincts it would be considered passé or gauche to attack an opponent as a "bleeding heart," but in some circumstances it might be useful to assure voters that you aren't one.

"I am not a *bleeding heart,* a sob sister." (Representative Geraldine A. Ferraro, 1982)

See also: *paternalism*

blessed land
USAGE: No need to employ as a description of any country other than the United States.

"I am addressing the heroes of whom I speak—you, the citizens of this *blessed land.*" (Ronald Reagan, January 20, 1981)

"To preserve our *blessed land,* we must look to God." (Ronald Reagan, February 9, 1982)

"But we, the present-day Americans, are not given to looking backward. In this *blessed land,* there is always a better tomorrow." (Ronald Reagan, January 21, 1985)

See also: *America, God bless the United States of; under God*

blood in the water
See: *feeding frenzy*

bloodied but unbowed
USAGE: Makes for fine TV and radio sound-bites in concession speeches.

Tonight I may be *bloodied but* I remain *unbowed*.

blow the whistle
After watching countless cop shows and football games on TV, many people can relate positively to this expression. Conditioned to acknowledge authority if not exactly respect it, voters may enjoy the idea that their elected representatives can order some bang-up police actions or penalties if need be.

"It is time to *blow the whistle* on Saddam Hussein." (Senator Alfonse M. D'Amato, January 12, 1991)

bodyguard of lies
In foreign policy matters, the ultimate public defense for deliberate deception of the American public by U.S. government officials.

Derivation: "In time of war," Winston Churchill declared, "the truth is so precious it must be attended by a *bodyguard of lies*."

See also: *lie*

bold
Intrepid and perhaps inspiring, while also managing to advance self-interest. A grown-up politician's version of "Look, Ma, no hands."

USAGE: "Bold" solicits admiration, usually stressing the glories of risk without its downsides.

"Because of America's *bold* initiatives, 1972 will be long remembered as the year of the greatest progress since the end of World War II toward a lasting peace in the world." (Richard M. Nixon, January 20, 1973)

"But our Democratic leaders have responded with *bold* and creative initiatives." (Representative Barbara Boxer, July 18, 1988)

"We must be equally *bold* in meeting both the capital deficit crisis of the newly developing democracies wherever they are in Eastern Europe, Latin America, Africa, or Asia and the overwhelming burdens of international debt in many of the same countries." (Senator Richard G. Lugar, January 17, 1991)

"Can we be *bold* and imaginative enough to create the conditions that will enhance our children's future?" (Senator Bill Bradley, April 15, 1991)

"I think it is perfectly legitimate for the president to say, 'Look, this success [the Gulf War] serves as evidence of strong and *bold,* courageous leadership provided by the Bush presidency,' and the country will give him enormous credit for it." (Senator Albert Gore, Jr., April 21, 1991)

Antonym: reckless
See also: *bite the bullet; leadership*

borders, porous
See: *aliens, illegal*

bow our heads in prayer
An invocation to set aside political matters in favor of spiritual unity.
USAGE: Reinforces images of humility and piety.

See also: *America, God bless the United States of; under God*

boys on the bus
An often contemptuous term for the press corps.
   No one elected the *boys on the bus*.
   See also: *herd journalism*

brainwashing
Mental manipulation and attempts at mind control by hostile powers.
   Derivation: Coined by CIA-employed journalist Edward Hunter during Korean War.

breakdown of the family
See: *family breakdown*

brie-and-white-wine set
Derisive term for people with money and refined tastes in an opposing political camp.
   Variations: brie-and-Chablis crowd; wine-and-cheese set

brilliant
Not as dull or mediocre as some others.
   "Mike Dukakis ran a *brilliant* campaign of substance and respect for the intelligence of the American people." (Jimmy Carter, July 18, 1988)
   See also: *dynamic*

bring our boys home
Withdraw U.S. troops from overseas involvement in a military conflict.
USAGE: Unusual, unless describing a *fait accompli*. This is one curve you probably won't ever choose to get in front of.

"The time has come to *bring our boys home. . . .*"
(Dwight D. Eisenhower, 1952)

broad-minded
Similar outlook.
USAGE: This term is itself so broad that it connotes nothing
other than implicit virtue.

The U.S. Supreme Court nominee being sought would be
"very *broad-minded* on the issues." (George Bush, June 28,
1991)

buck stops here, the
Outranks "Give 'em hell!" as the most cloying of oft-re-
peated Trumanisms. Numerous connotations, including: It's
lonely at the top; other politicians can/do pass the buck but
I can't/don't; what I say goes; nobody else could possibly
understand my trials and tribulations. Or, as an anti-incum-
bent theme: We need someone who'll be in charge.
USAGE: Presidential, gubernatorial and mayoral candidates
are well situated to get mileage out of this one.

"When President Truman was in the White House, there
was a sign on his desk. Remember what it said? *'The buck
stops here.'* There was never any doubt about who was captain of the ship. . . ." (Jimmy Carter, September 6, 1976)

"As Harry Truman said, *the buck does stop* with the President." (Senator Robert Dole, January 2, 1988)

buildup
New weaponry production and deployment, especially by
another government.
USAGE: This word is most suited for countries you wish to
portray as potential military threats. In such cases, never
use the innocent-sounding word "modernization," which is

to be reserved for buildups by the United States and its allies.

"One nation, the Soviet Union, has conducted the greatest military *buildup* in the history of man, building arsenals of awesome offensive weapons." (Ronald Reagan, January 21, 1985)

See also: *modernization*

bully
A rival in world affairs, willing to inflict human suffering to gain geopolitical advantage. To many people in the world the United States qualifies; this cannot be acknowledged by U.S. politicians, even—or especially—after the massive bombing of Iraq in early 1991.
USAGE: "Bully" evokes childhood memories for many Americans, and can be an effective word for engendering further resentment toward disliked leaders of other governments.

"From the U.S. standpoint, we can't allow this brutal *bully* [Saddam Hussein] to go back on this solemn agreement and to threaten people that are there under U.N. jurisdiction." (George Bush, June 28, 1991)

bureaucracy
Slow-moving, oafish, self-aggrandizing governmental agencies. An often amorphous whipping post always available for a righteous tongue-lashing.
USAGE: Everyone has felt anger and frustration at bureaucratic snafus. Since no one could be remotely in favor of "bureaucracy" as such, it is a no-lose target for rhetorical fire.

"The people is fed up with *bureaucracy*." (George Wallace, 1972)

"As a governor, I had to deal each day with the complicated and confused and overlapping and wasteful federal government *bureaucracy.*" (Jimmy Carter, July 15, 1976)

See also: *big government; bureaucrats; red tape*

bureaucratic nightmare

USAGE: You should encourage voters to think of you as someone striving to awaken everyone from such awful dreams.

"Whoever cooked up this *bureaucratic nightmare* inadvertently targeted some of the most hard-pressed people in Texas to impose it on: farmers, oil operators and fishermen." (Senator Phil Gramm, October 12, 1988)

bureaucrats

Personifications of bureaucracy. The villains of countless political tales.

USAGE: As much as possible, don't be specific when blasting "bureaucrats." Civil servants vote too.

"I think we ought to empower people who have been told for too long by *bureaucrats* what to do." (Arkansas governor Bill Clinton, June 15, 1991)

"It is all too easy for the government official to become a *bureaucrat.* It is all too easy to forget that ours is a government FOR the people and that those in government are in public service, not self-service." (Hubert H. Humphrey, December 8, 1965)

"When politics becomes the monopoly of the few and ceases to be the business of every citizen, the result is government by *bureaucrats,* by cronies and by machines." (Dwight D. Eisenhower, September 9, 1952)

See also: *bureaucracy*

business as usual
Status quo activities and policies that one wishes to criticize.
USAGE: This term is reserved for negative allusions. Ordinarily part of an attack on government, not on corporations.

"I simply will not sanction *business as usual.* I will not sanction the same type of unrealistic economic assumptions, poor accounting, and phantom spending cuts that have put us in this crisis in the first place." (Representative Tom Campbell, October 16, 1990)

Cc Dd

"C" is for Constituent Services
"D" is for Deterrence

called to greatness
USAGE: The religious undertones are apt to counteract any danger of sounding overblown. Thus, a grandiose way of sounding humble.

"I believe that we Americans are ready to be *called to greatness.*" (John F. Kennedy, January 1, 1960)
    See also: *greatness*

can-do
An upbeat tag for American attitudes and activities.
USAGE: Can put some zing in your lexicon, as you exude belief in the power of positive thinking.

"I believe our troops are telling us that we must not allow a great renewal of the American spirit to begin and end on foreign shores. They are telling us that we can apply the *can-do* spirit of the Persian Gulf conflict to the very serious problems facing us right here at home." (Senator Wendell H. Ford, June 22, 1991)

"It's time to rekindle the American spirit of invention and daring, to exchange voodoo economics for *can-do* economics, to build the best America by bringing out the best in every American." (Michael Dukakis, July 21, 1988)

See also: *voodoo*

caring

USAGE: Encourages people to make favorable assumptions that commit you to absolutely nothing, other than perhaps reminding them about this admirable personal internal condition of "caring"—hardly subject to empirical challenge.

"We can offer the American people in 1988 a committed, *caring* and concerned national ticket." (Democratic National Committee vice chair Polly Baca, (July 18, 1988)

"There is, as [Senator] Pete [Domenici] so eloquently said, in the American heart a spirit of love, of *caring,* and a willingness to work together." (Ronald Reagan, February 4, 1982)

See also: *neighbor caring for neighbor*

case-in-point

USAGE: When you want to portray a problem or scandal in the opposing camp as symptomatic.

Antonym: *aberration*

cash cow

If money is indeed the mother's milk of politics, then politicians tend to be selective in their outrage about instances of untoward milking.

"For too long, Federal research funds have been treated as a *cash cow* for the universities." (Representative John D. Dingell, May 9, 1991)

casualties
If Americans, sorrow. If "enemy" troops, elation. If "enemy" civilians, silence or excuses.

cathedral of the spirit
Raise high the holy rhetoric beam, carpenter.
". . . we can build a great *cathedral of the spirit*—each of us raising it one stone at a time, as he reaches out to his neighbor, helping, caring, doing." (Richard M. Nixon, January 20, 1969)
See also: *majesty*

caving in
Antonym: *pragmatism*

change for change's sake
A nice straw argument for straw argument's sake. Not too many people actually advocate "change for change's sake," but coming out against it is presumably an indication of laudable rationality.
"Unlike some, I do not believe in *change for change's sake*. But I am not opposed to changes if there is a real need, and the solution makes sense." (Representative John D. Dingell, February 26, 1991)

character
An amorphous dollop of purported virtue, easily ascribed to almost any fellow politician who is not a convicted felon. Considering the source, often a rather dubious plaudit.

Lloyd Bentsen is "a man of *character* and ability." (Senator Strom Thurmond, July 13, 1988)

character assassination
See: *smear; vendetta, personal*

cheap shot
An unappreciated salvo of verbiage; likely to be more resented the closer it is to the mark.

"As I listened to these accusations [by Jimmy Carter during the presidential debate of October 6, 1976], my resentment mounted almost to the breaking point. . . . This was a *cheap shot* at Kissinger and me and I should have said so. Furthermore, it wasn't true. Of course I got Henry's advice on foreign policy, but I made the decisions myself." (Gerald R. Ford, 1979)

"I think we're doing a marvelous job of explaining just how *cheap* a *shot* can get." (Representative Henry J. Hyde, June 25, 1991)

See also: *below the belt*

chemical dependency
Drug abuse among the upper classes.

civic-minded
Similarly minded.
    Antonym: *self-appointed*

civilized world
Amazing how uncivilized it can be.
USAGE: Referring to the United States and its current allies. Never acknowledge that today's enemy may have been part of yesterday's "civilized world."

"The President was wise to begin with an air attack on

Saddam's chemical and nuclear facilities and weapons. To me, Saddam's war-making ability has been of paramount concern. The *civilized world* must stop Saddam Hussein, and now is the time." (Representative Tom Campbell, January 16, 1991)

See also: *our allies*

clarify

USAGE: When some backtracking is in order, you can "clarify" earlier statements or actions.

See also: *misspoke*

class warfare

Aggravated class conflict. Roundly condemned by many a politician who actually supports it, as long as it's being waged from the top down.

"*Class warfare* is certainly good politics. But it's good politics at the expense of the nation's industrial base. Democrats should be concerned with what a targeted capital gains tax would do for America and not be focused on a myopic discourse about who benefits the most under such a system." (former senator Paul E. Tsongas, March 1991)

clean air

Cleaner than some other air.

"We should see a vast expansion in the use of natural gas in the next few years with the passage of a *Clean Air* Act next year." (Senator Phil Gramm, October 26, 1989)

"Together, these last two years, we've . . . [a]pplied the creativity of the marketplace in the service of the environment, for *clean air.*" (George Bush, January 29, 1991)

See also: *air quality*

cleanup

Minimal amelioration of the more obvious forms of pollution from toxic wastes, chemicals, radioactive isotopes, oil spills, and the like.

USAGE: Always say you're for a "cleanup" of any environmental disaster. Sounds nice, and probably won't ruffle any corporate feathers, since the term can stretch easily to cover the most superficial of cosmetic makeovers in the face of ecological catastrophes.

clear and present danger

The danger may actually be murky and off in the distance, or a mirage or fabrication, but "clear and present" sounds plenty dramatic.

"Let us react automatically, briskly and effectively to the threat of violent revolution and recognize it for the *clear and present danger* it constitutes." (Vice President Spiro T. Agnew, speaking about upheavals within the United States, to 1970 Governors Conference.)

coddling criminals

USAGE: Sounds like muggers, murderers, rapists, et al. are being tucked in each night under luxurious quilts, perhaps with a kiss on the forehead, and some graham crackers and warm milk on the night table.

cold war

Obsolete.

"There is but one sure way to avoid total war—and that is to win the *cold war*." (Dwight D. Eisenhower, February 2, 1953)

collateral damage
Wartime civilian deaths and injuries caused by the U.S. military and its allies.

Antonym: civilian victims of the monstrous brutality the United States is committed to stopping, etc.

color-conscious
USAGE: Claiming to be against "color-conscious" legislation can be a nifty verbal maneuver when you want to oppose redress of racism but you want to do so in the name of opposing racial discrimination. This one comes in very handy while attempting to block civil rights measures: Simply claim to be against laws and regulations that make any distinctions according to color; in that way you can impede corrective steps for long-standing racial bias even while preening yourself as a foe of racial bias.

"This bill will accomplish precisely what the 1964 civil rights bill stood four-square against—a *color-conscious* society. This bill codifies racial preference." (Representative Henry J. Hyde, June 4, 1991)

See also: *quotas*

command economy
An overtly commanded economy, rather than a more covertly and corporately manipulated economy.

Antonyms: *free enterprise system; market economy*

commander in chief
Heil to the chief.
USAGE: This moniker is especially helpful whenever you're supporting military actions that the president has ordered or wants to order. After all, you're just following the leader.

"Therefore, I believe, since I do not have any moral objection to what we are doing—I just thought it was less wise to do it this way than the way I preferred to do it—that it is my obligation to do all that I can to support the President and support the fighting women and men in the field. He is the *Commander in Chief.* We gave him the authority. We gave him the constitutional equivalent of a declaration of war. As the *Commander in Chief,* he is required to exercise that responsibility as he sees fit. I am not a military expert, and it would be presumptuous of me to suggest how that war, now that it is underway, should be conducted, and I will not. I will follow his lead and judgment on that." (Senator Joseph R. Biden, Jr., January 24, 1991)

commandos
Perpetrators of violent acts, such as kidnapping and murder, supported by the U.S. government.
USAGE: Cruel actions on behalf of a political goal you support are committed by "commandos." Cruel actions on behalf of a political goal you don't support are committed by "terrorists." Got it?
    "Israeli *commandos* captured Sheik Abdul Karim Obeid, the terrorist leader of an organization that targets both American and Israeli citizens for abduction and assassination. Israel might have expected praise. They got derision. Evidently we have become so accustomed to failure—so content with inertia—that we cannot even recognize success when it stares us in the face." (Senator Dan Coats, August 1989)
    Antonym: *terrorists*

common sense
USAGE: By insisting that you are attuned to it, in contrast to some other politicians, you can encourage constituents to project their interpretations of "common sense" onto you. One size fits all.

"I do not believe that any political campaign justifies the declaration of a moratorium on *common sense.*" (Dwight D. Eisenhower, October 19, 1956)

"It is time for America to . . . govern at home not by confusion and crisis but with grace and imagination and *common sense.* . . . The tragedy of Vietnam and Cambodia, the disgrace of Watergate, and the embarrassment of the CIA revelations could have been avoided if our government had simply reflected the sound judgment and good *common sense* and the high moral character of the American people." (Jimmy Carter, July 15, 1976)

"For four years, we have practiced the politics of *common sense* and we have never been distracted from our sense of common purpose." (Democratic National Committee chair Paul G. Kirk, Jr., July 18, 1988)

"And I respect old-fashioned *common sense*—and have no great love—and I have no great love for the imaginings of the social planners. You see, I like what's been tested and found to be true." (George Bush, August 18, 1988)

"I put a lot of faith in the *common sense* of the American people to ignore no-tax pledges from either party." (Representative Robert J. Mrazek, July 19, 1988)

"In voting against the failed socialistic policies of the past, I have effectively supported a positive alternative—*common sense* conservative policies that promote jobs, opportunity, and freedoms for our nation and its people. . . . The *common-sense* advice I receive from you helps me to vote in accordance with your wishes." (Representative Mel Hancock, December 1990)

"We know that the rising cost of environmental protection is also contributing to economic disruption. We fought for a *common-sense* approach to the Clear Air Act of 1990. We are still fighting to implement this act in ways that will benefit our environment without destroying a large part of the coal industry." (Senator Wendell H. Ford, June 22, 1991)

compartmented system
A setup where semi-plausible deniability is built into the system.
USAGE: If you find that a political ally has come under suspicion for nefarious activities that went on all around him or her, attribute his or her dubious innocence to bureaucratic structures.

"That's sometimes the way it works in a *compartmented system*." (George Bush, July 12, 1991, speaking of his nominee to head the CIA, Robert Gates.)

compassion
USAGE: If you'd like to take calluses off an image, you can't beat this as a humanizing platitude. In any case, to whatever extent you actually feel compassion, you may as well—perhaps at frequent intervals—proclaim that you do. Also, depending on what direction you wish to move your image, you may want to combine with an expression of toughness.

"If we are to live in a decent society, there is no substitute for *compassion*." (Lyndon B. Johnson, July 24, 1964)

"He [Hubert H. Humphrey] matches energy in the right with *compassion* for the needs of others." (Lyndon B. Johnson, August 26, 1964)

"The peace we seek to win is not victory over any other people, but the peace that comes 'with healing in its wings'; with *compassion* for those who have suffered; with understanding for those who have opposed us . . ." (Richard M. Nixon, January 20, 1969)

"Our party has not been perfect. We have made mistakes, and we have paid for them. But ours is a tradition of leadership and *compassion* and progress." (Jimmy Carter, July 15, 1976)

"We shall reflect the *compassion* that is so much a part of your makeup." (Ronald Reagan, January 20, 1981)

"Now, there is a place for the Federal Government in matters of social *compassion*. But our fundamental goals must be to reduce dependency and upgrade the dignity of those who are infirm or disadvantaged." (Ronald Reagan, January 21, 1985)

"The Dukakis-Bentsen ticket has the toughness to govern and the *compassion* to care about people." (Democratic National Committee chair Paul G. Kirk, Jr., July 18, 1988)

"If you talk about *compassion* but refuse to help those in need, your children will learn to look the other way." (George Bush, May 4, 1991)

"I have watched with a great deal of *compassion* the enormous economic adversity through which the people in this state have gone in the last several years." (Arkansas governor Bill Clinton, May 18, 1991)

compelled

Can figure into an expression of disembodied integrity, at once apologetic and resolute.

USAGE: A hint of regret as a sop for those who don't like what you're saying; at the same time, those who do can be encouraged to admire your adherence to conscience.

"We are *compelled* to set new priorities and to bring needed change when faced with an unprecedented gap between what state government receives in taxes and what we've been spending." (California governor Pete Wilson, January 10, 1991)

compete successfully
Usage: Almost any favored program can be said to help the nation to "compete successfully."

"The ability of this country to *compete successfully* in a global economy and to work with the other nations of the world depends more and more on our ability to communicate in languages other than our own." (Representative Leon E. Panetta, February 27, 1991)

competence
Usage: Of course, you'll never want to come out against "competence," but after Dukakis wagered on the concept and lost, you'd probably be ill advised to gamble on it as a campaign theme.

". . . this election is not about ideology; it's about *competence.*" (Michael Dukakis, July 21, 1988)

See also: *incompetence*

competition
"And a young leader from the Midwest challenged this Administration to strike its white flag of surrender on trade and to raise the American flag of *competition*. . . . I'm talking about Congressman Dick Gephardt." (Democratic National Committee chair Paul G. Kirk, Jr., July 18, 1988)

competitive
A much-touted aim for the national economy. Competitiveness is a cash-filled pot forever being chased to the end of the political blarney rainbow.
Usage: Whatever appropriations and tax policies you favor, it should be a cinch to insist that they hold the key to a "competitive" future for the nation.

"You don't become more *competitive* by spending more on consumption rather than investing in science and technology." (Senator Phil Gramm, May 4, 1987, denouncing efforts to increase funds for domestic programs.)

"We're sliding in this country, where our *competitive* ability is concerned. . . ." (Senator Albert Gore, Jr., April 21, 1991)

complex issue
Don't expect to make sense out of what I'm saying. Or, constituents probably wouldn't understand if I explained it to them, so I won't bother.
USAGE: When an emotional issue may get out of hand and make some people mad at you, calling it "complex" can help you to imply strongly that it's all too complicated for non-experts to comprehend. This attitude can serve as a firebreak to take some heat off you.

compromise
Can be the height of deft pragmatism or the depth of depravity.

confrontation, politics of
Assertiveness from a rival that threatens to screw up a politician's plans.

consent of the governed
USAGE: This venerable catchphrase can appeal to citizens who angrily believe that they are being governed without their consent. Meanwhile, a bit of Founding Fathers luster may rub off on you.

"It is time to check and reverse the growth of government, which shows signs of having grown beyond the *consent of the governed.*" (Ronald Reagan, January 20, 1981)

"Ours was the first nation to dedicate itself clearly to basic moral and philosophical principles: that all people are created equal and endowed with inalienable rights to life, liberty, and the pursuit of happiness, and that the power of government is derived from the *consent of the governed.*" (Jimmy Carter, July 15, 1976)

Derivation: Declaration of Independence, July 4, 1776. ("We hold these Truths to be self-evident, that all Men are created equal, that they are endowed by their Creator with certain unalienable Rights, that among these are Life, Liberty, and the Pursuit of Happiness—That to secure these Rights, Governments are instituted among Men, deriving their just Powers from the *Consent of the Governed.* . . .")

conservative
Antonym (sort of): *liberal*

constituent services
Maybe helping an elderly citizen to receive a Social Security check. Or—less likely to be advertised to the voters back home—helping a bank magnate get a federal regulator to back off.
Antonym: *influence peddling*

constituents
Voters.
Antonyms: *pressure group; special interests*

constructive
USAGE: A nice tag for whatever you favor.

consumer confidence
Consumers' willingness to go deeper into debt.

control of our border
Antonym: *borders, porous*
  See also: *aliens, illegal*

controversial
USAGE: A noncommittal word for acknowledging that many people are outspoken about an issue. If you aren't, maybe you can fill up time and space by talking about how "controversial" the matter is; hopefully you can deflect attention away from your fence-sitting.

corporate citizen
Makes a CEO at a Fortune 500 company sound like John Q. Public.

costly measures
See: *costly regulations*

costly regulations
USAGE: Describe any regulations you oppose as "costly."

costs and benefits
USAGE: Speaking in terms of cost/benefit ratios can make you sound reasonably astute and evenhanded. Keep the specifics blurry, though, so that your underlying priorities aren't too transparent.
  "I do not mean to imply that protection of the environment is not important. It is very important. However, the *costs and* the *benefits* of any environmental program must be balanced with our national energy policy." (Senator Wendell H. Ford, September 8, 1989)

counterinsurgency
Jargon for often-murderous efforts to prevent the overthrow of frequently despotic regimes in poor countries.

counterterrorism
Often, terrorism supported as distinct from terrorism deplored.

See also: *commandos; terrorists*

country above party
See: *bipartisan*

courage
USAGE: You'll probably want to speak about "courage" a lot. Talking about it in theory is so much easier—and far more enjoyable—than demonstrating it in practice.

"He [the president] must have the *courage* to stand against the pressures of the few for the good of the many." (Richard M. Nixon, July 28, 1960)

"It takes great *courage* to do what you think is right even though it may mean the end of your career and the dislike and criticism of your friends and neighbors." (John F. Kennedy, 1961)

"The true *courage* of this nuclear age lies in the quest for peace." (Lyndon B. Johnson, August 27, 1964)

"Tonight, with the wind at our backs, with friends at our sides and with *courage* in our hearts, the race to the finish line begins." (Michael Dukakis, July 21, 1988)

"We have less than seven weeks to come to an agreement on this budget. It will call for honesty, cooperation, commitment and *courage.*" (New York governor Mario M. Cuomo, February 13, 1991)

covert operation

U.S. government activities abroad, customarily involving bribery or murder, shielded from public scrutiny, and often kept entirely secret.

USAGE: When word gets out about these actions, you can denounce them while claiming you knew nothing about them at the time; if you support them, you can try to concoct a wide range of excuses for why they were kept secret.

"The reason we had to have a *covert operation* is we believed that the people who wanted to talk to us, their lives would be forfeited if the Ayatollah ever found out they were doing this." (Ronald Reagan, November 28, 1987)

cover-up
See: *lie*

crack
See: *drug problem*

cradle-to-grave
See: *socialized*

crime
USAGE: This is a hot-button word. Push it often. Concentrate on violent actions by individual criminals and not cold-blooded (sometimes deadly) decisions by corporate managers.

"*Crime* is a sore on the face of America. It is a menace on our streets. It is a drain on our cities. It is a corrupter of our youth. It is . . ." (Lyndon B. Johnson, September 8, 1965)

"The time has come to declare that *crime* is unacceptable in our nation. . . ." (Jimmy Carter, October 15, 1976)

crime in the streets
See: *afraid to walk the streets*

criminal neglect
Antonym: inadvertent oversight

crippling our economic future
Synonym: sapping our economic vitality

crisis of confidence
An ominous upsurge of perceptiveness among the general public.

"Our nation is facing not only an economic crisis but also a *crisis of confidence*. Lack of action on the deficit has . . . planted serious doubt in the minds of the American people about the ability of the President and the Congress to govern this nation." (House Budget Committee chair Leon E. Panetta, October 27, 1990)

See also: *public cynicism; self-confidence; self-doubt*

critical mass
Some kind of political explosion that powers-that-be wouldn't like.

"Unless we act now to meet these goals, we could find ourselves with a *critical mass* of our citizens demanding a total government takeover of health care." (Secretary of Health and Human Services Louis W. Sullivan, June 23, 1991, urging the American Medical Association to limit increases in medical costs.)

crossroads of history
Whatever the calendars and watches are saying, we're always there. A kind of rhetorical gridlock.

"I believe we are really at the *crossroads of history*." (Representative William S. Broomfield, January 12, 1991)

See also: *threshold*

cruelest tax, the
Synonym: inflation

daddy
USAGE: Fond reminiscences, hopefully endearing you to audiences.

". . . and we listened to the grown-ups talk. I can still hear the sound of the dominoes clicking on the marble slab my *daddy* had found for a tabletop." (Texas State treasurer Ann W. Richards, July 18, 1988)

Caution: On the other hand, extensive anecdotes about mothers may be more problematic for politicians of either gender; a risk is that such reminiscences might convey a yearning for "mommy" and thus make male speakers sound less masculine and female speakers appear stereotypically weak.

See also: *America, the promise of; profamily; values, family*

dead
An expired condition, but not necessarily a disqualifier for public office.

"Had he not dropped *dead* while campaigning, he would have won easily. If our campaign to re-elect him is successful, the committee would come up with a replacement who can carry forth his goals and ideals." (John D. Hughes, member of the Republican Party Committee for Upper Providence Township in Pennsylvania, May 1991)

"I respect Mr. Kershner, and I don't mention that he is *dead* unless people ask me about it." (Howard P. Huber, Jr., candidate running against the late Robert Kershner for the Upper Providence Township board of supervisors, May 1991)

debt ceiling
The limit imposed on government debt, made to sound final but actually moving skyward with the help of rhetorical cranes and winches.
   See also: *Gramm-Rudman*

debt crisis
In international lending there are actually two debt crises—one besets poor people in Third World countries, the other affects banks in places like midtown Manhattan. Since U.S. politicians are much more likely to care about what banks think of them, the boardroom perspectives favoring "austerity measures" for the poor are apt to dominate politicians' views of the "debt crisis."
   See also: *austerity measures*

debtor nation
Often uttered in stage-whispered anguish or horrified exclamation, this sobriquet is calculated to stick in the craw of self-respecting Americans.
Usage: The notion of America the Deadbeat is one you'll probably want to use sparingly. Whatever causative theory you choose to espouse from among the hundreds available, you should take the opportunity to ascribe "debtor nation" status to the ascendancy of certain policies advanced by particular politicians. No need to mention the connections with high military spending. Preferred phrasing includes the words "gone from being" to underscore the deterioration at hand.
   ". . . consider that in less than ten years time we have gone from being a net creditor nation to being the world's

largest (in absolute amounts) net *debtor nation*." (Representative Helen Delich Bentley, 1991)

"The U.S. has gone from being the largest lending nation in the world to the largest *debtor nation* in history." (Representative John Bryant, 1991)

"We were never meant to be the world's greatest *debtor nation*." (former senator Paul E. Tsongas, April 30, 1991)

Antonym: *number one*

See also: *national debt*

decency

Whatever the viewer/listener/reader assumes to be at least minimally acceptable standards of human conduct.

"The best foreign policy is to live our daily lives in honesty, *decency* and integrity . . ." (Dwight D. Eisenhower, April 1950)

"When we listen to 'the better angels of our nature,' we find that they celebrate the simple things, the basic things—such as goodness, *decency,* love, kindness." (Richard M. Nixon, January 20, 1969)

"We do not seek to intimidate, but it is clear that a world which others can dominate with impunity would be inhospitable to *decency* and a threat to the well-being of all people." (Jimmy Carter, January 20, 1977)

"The Party of working men and women will bestow its highest honor upon the son of Greek immigrants. His life is one of *decency* and diligence." (Democratic National Committee chair Paul G. Kirk, Jr., July 18, 1988)

". . . we must have a foreign policy that reflects the *decency* and the principles and the values of the American people." (Michael Dukakis, July 21, 1988)

declared war on the United States

Almost always metaphorically.

USAGE: Although many world leaders at one time or another issue rhetorical declarations of war, you might find it helpful to take such oratorical hyperboles literally to depict U.S. initiation of military action as preemptive.

"I wouldn't have hesitated to kill him [Qadhafi]. He's a madman and he was a terrorist and he *declared war on the United States*." (Pat Robertson, February 13, 1988)

See also: *madman*

decline

USAGE: Anyone referring to negative national trends can be assailed for noting, and thus being resigned to, "decline."

"We are not, as some would have us believe, doomed to an inevitable *decline*." (Ronald Reagan, January 20, 1981)

"My opponent's view of the world sees a long, slow *decline* for our country, an inevitable fall mandated by impersonal historical forces. But America is not in *decline*. America is a rising nation." (George Bush, August 18, 1988)

"America is not the casual acceptance of economic *decline* and social disintegration. Yet, that is what some are prepared to endure." (former senator Paul E. Tsongas, March 1991)

Antonym: *renewal*

defense

USAGE: The best way to describe U.S. military aims, no matter what.

"Arms are solely for *defense*—to protect from violent assault what we already have." (Dwight D. Eisenhower, April 21, 1956)

"So far as we are concerned, the amassing of military might never has been—and never will be—devoted to any other end than *defense* and the preservation of a just peace." (Dwight D. Eisenhower, November 7, 1957)

"In the past five years, our Administration has reversed the decline in *defense* funding that occurred during the 1970s. . . ." (Ronald Reagan, February 6, 1986)

defense spending

Military spending.

USAGE: A good defense for military spending is always to refer to it as "defense spending."

"Jimmy Carter . . . pledged real increases in *defense spending* and persuaded his NATO partners to do the same." (former secretary of state Edmund S. Muskie, July 18, 1988)

defensive

When a president stresses that the deployment of U.S. troops is for "defensive" purposes, the Pentagon's attack plans are often in high gear.

"America does not seek conflict, nor do we seek to chart the destiny of other nations. But America will stand by her friends. The mission of our troops is wholly *defensive*." (George Bush, August 8, 1990)

deficit, the

USAGE: "The deficit" is the economic Antichrist of U.S. political theology, so you must always find it appalling. Treat it as a symbol of fiscal evil; keep proclaiming that you're aghast and determined to reverse the demise of the nation's financial virtue.

deficit spending

Trafficking with a devilish troll who dwells under fiscal bridges.

"I believe deeply that continuing *deficit spending* is immoral." (Dwight D. Eisenhower, June 1, 1961)

Antonym: *pay-as-you-go*

demagoguery

Dishonest oratory pandering to the worst of human prejudices—unless it's oratory coming from one's own side. Of course, there's nothing to stop a demagogue from engaging in long and loud denunciations of "demagoguery."

USAGE: When an opponent is really getting on your nerves, try condemning "demagoguery" while proclaiming your lofty preoccupations.

"In the light of our world position, our nation cannot tolerate, in any individual or in any party, *demagoguery* that would put winning a cheap political advantage above winning the world struggle for justice and freedom." (Dwight D. Eisenhower, March 18, 1958)

"That cheap political *demagoguery* got my goat, and I became strident in return." (Gerald R. Ford, 1979)

democracy

Commonly a system where each adult has a vote, and the wealthy have more powerful ways to determine government policies.

"*Democracy* rests on the voice of the people." (Lyndon B. Johnson, May 25, 1967)

"Meanwhile, the government of El Salvador, making every effort to guarantee *democracy,* free labor unions, freedom of religion, and a free press, is under attack by guerrillas. . . ." (Ronald Reagan, April 27, 1983)

"Ninety-nine percent of the people of this hemisphere live either in a *democracy* or a country that is on the road to *democracy*. One percent live under the hemisphere's last dictator, Fidel Castro." (George Bush, May 20, 1991)

Democrat-controlled Congress
USAGE: By opponents of the Democratic Party.

Democrat Party
USAGE: If you're a Republican you'll want to drop the "ic."

"The *Democrat Party* is not one—but two—political parties with the same name. They unite only once every two years—to wage political campaigns." (Dwight D. Eisenhower, October 20, 1958)

Democratic-led Congress
USAGE: By supporters of the Democratic Party.

Desert Storms
Glorious prospective crusades in which the United States can and should expect to vanquish various foes at little cost other than massive human suffering among people who live in countries run by geopolitical infidels of the moment.
USAGE: An allegorical metaphor for upcoming grand-scale national triumphs that should be looked forward to with proud anticipation. If properly injected by your speeches and press releases, this term should have an adrenally patriotic effect.

"I honestly believe, if we don't do something to turn this situation around, ten or twenty years from now, you won't have the America that you grew up in. The idea of equality will be gone. We'll be a two-tiered society that will be a joke compared to our former selves, and we will not be leading the *Desert Storms* in the 21st century." (Arkansas governor Bill Clinton, May 18, 1991)

destiny
Often the high-blown destination for the national path.

"Democrats cannot be trusted to define the *destiny* of America. . . ." (Senator Phil Gramm, February 28, 1991)

destruction was mutual, the
USAGE: If asked why the U.S. government failed to provide major assistance to a country it has ravaged with massive and protracted bombardment, you can say something like "the destruction was mutual." The American press corps is unlikely to challenge such a statement.

". . . *the destruction was mutual.*" (Jimmy Carter, March 24, 1977, giving his reason why the United States had no responsibility to provide aid to Vietnam in the wake of the Vietnam War.)

deterrence
The purported purpose and effect of nuclear weapons in the U.S. arsenal. In contrast, American politicians are careful not to apply the soothing upbeat word "deterrence" to nuclear weapons pointed at the United States.
USAGE: If constituents seem jumpy about nuclear arsenals, just talk about "deterrence" for a while and that may calm them down.

"The Alliance has carried its strength not as a battle flag, but as a banner of peace. *Deterrence* has kept that peace, and we must continue to take the steps necessary to make *deterrence* credible." (Ronald Reagan, June 9, 1982)

"America's *deterrence* is more credible, and it is making the world a safer place—safer because now there is less danger that the Soviet leadership will underestimate our strength or question our resolve." (Ronald Reagan, January 16, 1984)

See also: *military preparedness; modernization; resolve*

device
Tidy euphemism for a U.S. nuclear bomb.

devoted to his wife and children
USAGE: Never hurts. Be sure, however, that the man you're describing is not separated, divorced, or single.

". . . the kind of man who plays it straight, keeps his word and pays his bills . . . *devoted to his wife and children*." (Arkansas governor Bill Clinton, July 20, 1988, describing Michael Dukakis.)

dictate
USAGE: When you want to prevent certain people from gaining more power, say that they want to be able to "dictate."

"This bill would foster labor unrest in the small business community. It would allow unions working with just two employees to *dictate* to an employer the workplace policies of his or her business." (Representative Andy Ireland, July 10, 1991)

dignity
A reliable esteem engine for the verbiage track.

Americans should "respect the life and the *dignity* of every human being." (George Bush, January 14, 1991, two days before U.S. missiles were first launched against Iraq.)

"Freedom and the *dignity* of the individual have been more available and assured here than in any other place on Earth." (Ronald Reagan, January 20, 1981)

"Our commitment to human rights must be absolute, our laws fair, our natural beauty preserved; the powerful must not persecute the weak, and human *dignity* must be enhanced." (Jimmy Carter, January 20, 1977)

"The most intangible, but most important, direction in

which we need to move is toward the enhancement of human *dignity*." (Hubert H. Humphrey, June 16, 1966)

"A fundamental belief shines forth in this Republic. We believe in the worth and *dignity* of the individual." (Dwight D. Eisenhower, January 5, 1956)

"It is our faith in human *dignity* that underlies our purposes." (Harry S Truman, January 7, 1948)

diplomacy
A wide range of international nonmilitary efforts, ranging from the sincere and forthright to the disingenuous and devious.

"We must put effort, skill and faith in our *diplomacy* . . . for upon it, ultimately, will depend the prevention of World War III." (Dwight D. Eisenhower, September 19, 1956)

"*Diplomacy* and defense are no longer distinct alternatives, one to be used where the other fails; each must complement the other." (John F. Kennedy, March 28, 1961)

"I know that peace does not come through wishing for it —that there is no substitute for days and even years of patient and prolonged *diplomacy*." (Richard M. Nixon, January 20, 1969)

"Most recently, President Bush offered Saddam a chance for face-to-face *diplomacy*." (Representative William S. Broomfield, January 11, 1991)

"The tactics of terror lead nowhere—there can be no substitute for *diplomacy*." (George Bush, March 6, 1991)

dirty tricks
Political maneuvers that are (a) sneaky, (b) uncovered, and (c) done by the other side.

Antonym: *hardball politics*

disadvantaged

Euphemism for oppressed and discriminated against.

"But our fundamental goals must be to reduce dependency and upgrade the dignity of those who are infirm or *disadvantaged*." (Ronald Reagan, January 21, 1985)

"In Idaho, as in much of the Western United States, people see these systems and their abysmal results as evidence of the wrongheadedness of our approaches to the problems they are designed to solve. These folks will contend that the answer is not for government to help the *disadvantaged* even more, but rather for government simply to get out of the way and encourage the *disadvantaged* to see their potential and to reach it." (Representative Larry Craig, July 30, 1991)

See also: *less fortunate; underprivileged*

disastrous policies

See: *bankrupt policies*

disgruntled former employee

USAGE: This is an ideal way to refer to any ex-aide who generates negative publicity about you.

divisive

Stubborn instead of pliable.

"After years of bitter controversy and *divisive* national debate, I have been advised and I am compelled to conclude that many months and perhaps more years will have to pass before Richard Nixon could obtain a fair trial by jury in any jurisdiction of the United States. . . ." (Gerald R. Ford, September 8, 1974)

Synonym: *polarizing*

divisiveness
Often a pejorative for candid confrontation of inequities.
USAGE: If a proposed change in the status quo would force certain people to cede some power to people with less of it, posing as an opponent of such "divisiveness" can ingratiate you with the powerful.

The administration's bill "stresses fairness over quotas, conciliation over litigation, unity over *divisiveness.*" (Representative Robert H. Michel, June 4, 1991)

doomsayers
Antonym: *hope, apostle of*
See also: *naysayers; prophets of doom*

downturn, serious
Economic setbacks, described by administration detractors.

downturn, temporary
Economic setbacks, described by administration supporters.

dreams can come true for all of us
USAGE: A quick trip to a political Magic Kingdom. This is a good way to infantilize voters; many of them seem to want to believe the stuff of Walt Disney tunes, and they may appreciate the sentiment. Remember, plenty of people casting their ballots also participate in another government-sponsored activity—buying lottery tickets.

"I stand before you to proclaim tonight: America is a land where *dreams can come true for all of us.*" (Geraldine Ferraro, July 19, 1984, speaking to the Democratic National Convention as the vice presidential nominee.)

See also: *magic of America*

drug culture
A selective and disparaging reference to social contexts of certain illegal drugs.

"It should not be surprising, then, that in recent years so many young people have been drawn into the *drug culture*. It is, after all, the 'in' thing to do among their friends. And it has been urged on them by some of their pop heroes." (Spiro Agnew, September 14, 1970)

See also: *drugs*

drug-free America
The nation's biggest and most dangerous drug pushers—tobacco companies and alcohol sellers—have no reason to fear calls for a "drug-free America" by politicians who wouldn't dream of taking on the cigarette and booze industries.

"I want a *drug-free America*—and this will not be easy to achieve. But . . ." (George Bush, August 18, 1988)

"The fight for a *drug-free America* has not been tried and found wanting. It has been tried and found difficult." (Senator Dan Coats, 1989)

drug kingpins
Not Philip Morris or Adolph Coors or Jack Daniels.

"In 1988, I voted for the death penalty when applied to *drug kingpins*." (Senator Dan Coats, 1989)

drug problem
Use of illegal drugs, not of alcohol, cigarettes, and over-prescribed pharmaceuticals.

drugs
In political parlance, only those "drugs" that are illegal.

"This year, I will propose a Drug Control Act to provide

stricter penalties for those who traffic in LSD and other dangerous *drugs* with our people." (Lyndon B. Johnson, January 17, 1968)

See also: *war on drugs*

dupes
See: *stooges*

dynamic
A run-of-the-mill superlative.
USAGE: Due to chronic hyperinflation of rhetoric, most suitable as routine praise.

"Under the leadership of Paul Kirk, the Democratic National Committee is a *dynamic* organization." (Georgia Democratic Party chair John Henry Anderson, July 18, 1988)

"Paul Kirk has put this Party on a sound financial basis. He's forged a *dynamic* working relationship between grassroots Democrats and our elected officials." (Democratic National Convention Rules Committee chair Kathleen M. Vick, July 18, 1988)

"Last, but certainly not least, is the *dynamic* Mayor of Little Rock, Arkansas, Lottie Shackelford. . . ." (Representative Martin Frost, July 18, 1988)

See also: *brilliant; great*

Ee Ff

"E" is for Empower
"F" is for Founding Fathers

E Pluribus Unum

USAGE: A Latin maxim can seem authoritative—this one especially, since it's linked with money.

"And where we debate, it is to reach consensus in the pursuit of the motto minted on our coinage, '*E Pluribus Unum*,' from many one, one as a Party, one as a people, one as a Nation." (Fulton County, Georgia, commissioner Michael Lomax, July 18, 1988)

"For the last four years the Democratic Party has demonstrated that diversity and the politics of inclusion are a true reflection of the character—yes the motto of this Republic that we love so well, '*E Pluribus Unum*'—one from many." (Democratic National Committee chair Paul G. Kirk, Jr., July 18, 1988)

eagle's wings

Patriotic ornithology taking to rhetorical flight.
USAGE: Hopefully flag-wavers and environmentalists can relate.

"You heard a young Senator urge us to honor our heroes by daring to dream again as they did. He reminded us that we could raise ourselves up on *eagle's wings* to new heights as Americans. . . . Let us hear a cheer for Senator Joe Biden of Delaware." (Democratic National Committee chair Paul G. Kirk, Jr., July 18, 1988)

easy answers
A phrase that's useful while trying to give the impression that no better remedies are available than what voters are hearing at the moment.

"In this next decade there are not going to be any *easy answers.*" (John F. Kennedy, January 1, 1960)

"We must face the fact that there is no quick or *easy answer* to Vietnam." (Robert F. Kennedy, April 27, 1966)

"There are no *easy answers.* No single option we discuss for achieving Saddam Hussein's withdrawal from Kuwait holds a monopoly on merit." (Senator Warren B. Rudman, January 12, 1991)

economic barriers
Virtually any of the government's fiscal policies that the speaker doesn't like.

"The time has come for a new American emancipation— a great national drive to tear down *economic barriers* and liberate the spirit of enterprise in the most distressed areas of our country." (Ronald Reagan, January 21, 1985)

See also: *restrictions on the economy*

economic chaos
Actually, the economic conditions may have been carefully orchestrated rather than chaotic for the corporate strategists standing to gain from layoffs, shutdowns, etc. But "economic chaos" sounds like no blame could be affixed anywhere.

"We need to be creative and fight for ways to help our timber mills survive *economic chaos*—and the bill I'm introducing today is one way to do that." (Representative Jolene Unsoeld, June 26, 1991)

economic cure

Often the easing of inflation with a recessionary palliative.
USAGE: If you tell people they're swallowing an "economic cure," maybe even some laid-off workers will simmer down.

economic disaster

Customarily, what's in store if one's prescriptions for the economy are not implemented in short order.

"Without an energy policy to set the framework, it would be very easy, in the name of the environment, to close off some domestic energy options before an energy policy is even formulated. We must keep our options open. To do otherwise would render an *economic disaster.*" (Senator Wendell H. Ford, September 8, 1989)

"Our Northwest timber communities are facing a problem as gut-wrenching as any I've seen. Reduced harvests, partly due to protection for the Northern spotted owl, are triggering an *economic disaster* every bit as serious as that of the Great Depression." (Representative Jolene Unsoeld, June 26, 1991)

economic expansion

USAGE: This phrase aids efforts to intimidate people into accepting the idea that no matter how much their personal financial picture has deteriorated in recent years, it is anomalous in the context of the overall economy.

"We have . . . had the longest period of *economic expansion* in our nation's history . . . with 14 million new jobs since we've been here. That's more new jobs than Europe and Japan combined have produced in the last 10 years." (Ronald Reagan, November 28, 1987)

See also: *affluent society*

education

As a matter of course, virtually all politicians profess fervent belief in its vital importance.

"*Education* is the key to the growth of this country." (John F. Kennedy, November 15, 1963)

"*Education* is the keystone in the arch of man's freedom." (Hubert H. Humphrey, July 21, 1965)

"*Education* is the key to the future for every one of our children." (Robert F. Kennedy, October 21, 1966)

education reform

USAGE: Since almost everyone thinks that "education" needs "reform," you can't lose with this one, unless you get very specific—and why would you want to do a thing like that?

egghead

Too much of a thinker and not enough of a glad-hander.

"He's an *egghead* type, and I don't mean that disrespectfully. I just don't see Harris Wofford as having the personality to shake hands and rub elbows." (Pennsylvania State Senate president pro tem Robert C. Jubelirer, May 1991)

See also: *intellectuals, pointy-headed*

elite

USAGE: Of course you should only attack the "elite" who aren't in your political corner.

empower

Often used as a one-word oxymoron, in the process of proposing that people with power take steps to "empower" people who lack power. "Empower" often ends up as a condescending verb for reinforcing power relationships extant in the status quo.

USAGE: You can mix your messages nicely by declaring that you want to "empower" people while you convey that they can depend on you to empower them.

"I think we ought to *empower* people who have been told for too long by bureaucrats what to do." (Arkansas governor Bill Clinton, June 15, 1991)

"Homeownership is just one area in which President Bush is pushing the new approach of *empowerment.*" (Representative Harris W. Fawell, July 15, 1991)

"In the nineties we need to replace what resulted in 'free-enterprise for the few' with a more progressive approach to economic growth that *empowers* ALL Americans —not just those at the top—to participate and prosper in our economy. . . ." (New York governor Mario M. Cuomo, August 9, 1991)

empty feel-good rhetoric
A rhetorical put-down of competing rhetoric.
USAGE: When facing moral arguments, impugn the importance of feelings and imply that they are inappropriate for guiding policy.

"President Bush defended his renewal of trade benefits for China before an Asian-American audience today, saying he was more interested in reform in Beijing than '*empty feel-good rhetoric*' about its human rights abuses." (Associated Press, June 16, 1991)

end-game
Jockeying to wind up in a position to administer a *coup de grâce* or to hold a dominant position.
USAGE: Can make you sound like a geopolitically sophisticated chess player, akin to Henry Kissinger without a for-

eign accent. Since chess was invented as a metaphor for war, why not return the favor?

See also: *win the peace*

enemies of the country
An elastic definition, many times ludicrously stretched to suit powers that be, with murderous results.

Proclamation—"authorizing all citizens of Colorado, either individually or in such parties as they may organize, to go in pursuit of all hostile Indians on the plains, scrupulously avoiding those who have responded to my call to rendez-vous at the points indicated; also to kill and destroy as *enemies of the country* wherever they may be found, all such hostile Indians." (Colorado Territory governor John Evans, August 1864)

energy independence
See: *energy security*

energy security
Dependable reliance on favored sources of energy.
USAGE: The policy you advocate is the only path toward "energy security."

". . . the *energy security* of the U.S. and the world is at risk from the threat of a ruthless scoundrel such as Saddam Hussein." (Representative John D. Dingell, February 26, 1991)

"I don't have to tell you that we can never have economic security without *energy security*. And I don't have to tell you that we can never have *energy security* without coal—our most abundant source of domestic energy." (Senator Wendell H. Ford, June 22, 1991)

Antonym: *reliance on Mideast oil*

engagement
Often a euphemism for ongoing support of brutal regimes.

"Only by continued American *engagement* can we support moderation in El Salvador and convince the guerrillas that murder will not win the war—either in San Salvador or on Capitol Hill." (Dan Quayle, July 16, 1989)

enhanced
Benign, no matter how dangerous.

The United States will "keep an *enhanced* naval presence" in the Persian Gulf. (General Colin L. Powell, April 26, 1991)

enhancing the role of the individual
Cutting social programs so that more people will have to fend for themselves.

"One, we will provide for a stronger common defense; two, we will promote the general welfare by reducing the role of the federal government and *enhancing the role of the individual* in creating jobs; and, three, we will reduce the individual tax rate so that a person can keep a little more of the extra dollars his extra effort earns for him." (Representative Guy Vander Jagt, March 27, 1987)

See also: *big government; market economy; rising tide will lift all boats, a; voluntarism*

enlightened
USAGE: You're talking USA all the way.

"America is the most prosperous, productive, *enlightened* Nation on Earth—a nation that can do anything." (George Bush, June 12, 1991)

enshrined

USAGE: When you want to contend that a legal provision is of preeminent importance, or when ultimate reverence is called for, say that it is "enshrined." After all, people are reticent about messing with shrines.

Enshrined in our Constitution.

"The Constitution and the Declaration can live only as long as they are *enshrined* in our hearts and minds. If they are not so *enshrined,* they would be no better than mummies in their glass cases, and they could in time become idols whose worship would be a grim mockery of the true faith." (Dwight D. Eisenhower, December 15, 1952)

entrepreneurial genius

Clever ability to build profitable businesses.

USAGE: Handy for blurring distinctions between small companies and huge semimonopolistic firms. Since many people are sympathetic to the former and wary of the latter, you can provide a service to corporate contributors by lumping together such enterprises as an independent corner grocery store and the megacorporate Safeway chain.

"Freedom and incentives unleash the drive and *entrepreneurial genius* that are the core of human progress." (Ronald Reagan, January 21, 1985)

See also: *free enterprise system*

environment, the

USAGE: Just about everyone is in favor of it as a platitude, so you may as well give it lip service if nothing else.

environmental terrorism

A term not applied to such U.S.-based activities as atomic reactor operations, nuclear weapons production, thermonuclear warhead test explosions, chemical dumping, toxic pollution of waterways, and the like.

"But the world has to wonder what the dictator of Iraq is thinking. . . . If he thinks that he will advance his cause through tragic and despicable *environmental terrorism*—he is dead wrong." (George Bush, January 29, 1991)

equal opportunity
See: *color-conscious; opportunity; quotas*

equality
Easier said than won.

"*Equality* is the basic concept of our whole Government —we must never forget it." (Dwight D. Eisenhower, June 14, 1952)

"*Equality* to us is basically a religious ideal." (Richard M. Nixon, October 18, 1956)

escalate
Generally, what the other side does in military confrontations.

Antonyms: enhance security arrangements; modernize

ethics
Not getting linked to shady financial transactions, overt influence peddling, plagiarism of speeches, extramarital affairs, cheating back in college, etc.
USAGE: The operative political definition is so narrow that few subjects are discussed as ethical matters. You won't have to worry about having your "ethics" impugned if, for instance, you countenance racial or gender discrimination, or accept the suffering of huge numbers of poor children due to inadequate nutrition, housing, and health care; "ethics" in political parlance does not relate to such matters.

"I think you have to have enough experience to make intelligent decisions. You have to be able to listen, and then you have to be able to make decisions. But the decisions have to come from a personal conviction, a personal commitment. But throughout it all, there has to be *ethics,* there has to be character, there has to be leadership." (George Bush, December 5, 1987)

ethics reform
USAGE: The elasticity of this term is reflected in a *Los Angeles Times* news account of June 18, 1991. "Until recently, it was illegal for top administration officials to accept free travel from American corporations. But the law was changed to permit such trips at the request of President Bush as part of the so-called Ethics Reform Act, enacted in late 1989."
See also: *reforms*

evenhanded
Noncommittal; evasive.

every possible point of view
Doubtful. Much more likely the gamut from A to C.
"I have been an intent student of these events; at hearings and briefings where *every possible point of view* was exchanged by representatives of the Administration, and by experts of every kind; in the huge outpouring of information and opinion that the media bring us; in the views of many hundreds of my constituents, indeed thousands; and, finally, from this debate." (Senator Albert Gore, Jr., January 12, 1991, discussing authorization for a U.S. military attack on Iraq.)

everything we stand for
This self-satisfied expression has a blurry double meaning. What we think we "stand for"—or what others might reasonably perceive we "stand for." Politicians and their speechwriters are pleased to pretend there is no distinction.

"No arms for hostages. I think it runs against the grain of *everything we stand for* in America." (Senator Robert Dole, January 2, 1988)

See also: *American way, the*

evidence
Often vague, nonexistent, or based on the say-so of officials apt to substitute assertion for substantiation.

"The U.S. government has *evidence* that terrorists supported by Iraq are planning to mount attacks in most regions of the world." (Representative Dante Fascell, January 17, 1991)

"Whether Senator [Joseph] McCarthy has legal *evidence*, whether he has overstated or understated his case, is of lesser importance. The question is whether the Communist influence in the State Department still exists." (Senator Robert A. Taft, 1950)

evidence, available
An idiomatic escape hatch for possible later use if wrongdoing by a political ally becomes undeniable.

See also: *ambiguity; appearance of improprieties; compartmented system; feeding frenzy*

Evil Empire
Obsolete.

excited

A flattering claim of enthusiasm.

"I'm *excited*. I don't know if you get as *excited* as I do, but whenever I get a little discouraged I say to Muriel, 'Why don't we take a trip to Israel and get pumped up again?'" (Hubert H. Humphrey, 1972, speaking to the American Friends of Hebrew University in Philadelphia.)

expansionist

Trying to extend influence in other countries without approval from the United States.

"There is no question that the Soviet Union is *expansionist*." (Pierre S. du Pont IV, January 16, 1988)

expect no less

USAGE: When you are insisting that action must be taken to right past wrongs, you can always issue a ringing declaration that the people of the nation "expect no less." Actually, opinion polls often show quite the contrary—many citizens expect a lot less than adequate protection of their interests by the government—but it wouldn't do to close a speech by proclaiming that "people expect a lot less but let's surprise them"!

"Mr. Speaker, my bill is an important initiative to give the Justice Department and the independent prosecutor the time needed to pursue the criminal investigations of wrongdoing at HUD, and to demonstrate the commitment of Congress to redress this debacle. The American people *expect no less*." (Representative Tom Campbell, January 28, 1991)

expedient

USAGE: Some politicians, you are sad to say, make a practice of doing what's "expedient"—but you have a very different approach.

"My philosophy has always been: don't lean with the wind. Don't do what is politically *expedient*. Do what your instinct tells you is right." (Richard M. Nixon, 1962)

expert opinion

USAGE: Expert opinion that concurs with your opinion.

exporting American jobs

USAGE: A good way to imply that foreign countries are to blame for unemployment in the United States.

"Today we are *exporting American jobs* at an alarming rate and importing almost everything else, even our food." (Representative John Bryant, 1991)

See also: *debtor nation*

extremism

In the eyes of the beholder.

"The outcome of the Goldwater Convention in San Francisco was a flat refusal to repudiate *extremism*." (Hubert H. Humphrey, October 28, 1964)

"The recent riots in Chicago, Cleveland, New York and Omaha have produced in the public dialogue too much heat and very little light. The *extremists* have held the floor for too long. One extreme sees a simple remedy for rioting in a ruthless application of the truncheon and an earlier call to the National Guard. The other *extremists* are more articulate, but their position is equally simplistic. To them, riots are to be excused upon the grounds that the participants have legitimate social grievances or seek justifiable social goals." (Richard M. Nixon, August 15, 1966)

See also: *radical*

fair play
USAGE: No matter what your objective, the stroking of national self-image can be a real plus along the way.

"With the idealism and *fair play* which are the core of our system and our strength, we can have a strong and prosperous America at peace with itself and the world." (Ronald Reagan, January 20, 1981)

"Now, we Democrats believe that America is still the country of *fair play,* that we can come out of a small town or a poor neighborhood and have the same chance as anyone else, and it doesn't matter whether we are black or Hispanic or disabled or women." (Texas State treasurer Ann W. Richards, July 18, 1988)

". . . stalling on this issue would be downright unfair. It violates the very sense of *fair play* and honest dealing that should characterize our foreign policy. I believe you will agree with me that we should deal honestly with the South African Government and lift the sanctions now." (Representative William S. Broomfield, June 25, 1991)

See also: *level playing field*

fair to the whole country
Expedient for winning the next national election.

"Nobody wants a civil rights bill more than George Bush. But he wants one that's *fair to the whole country.*" (Barbara Bush, June 6, 1991)

fairies
A term that preens one's manliness while imputing insufficient heterosexuality to other men.

"After Vietnam, we had a cottage industry developed in Washington, D.C., consisting of a bunch of military *fairies* that had never been shot at in anger [and] who felt fully qualified to comment on the leadership abilities of all the leaders of the U.S. Army." (General Norman Schwarzkopf, May 1991)

Caution: Inadvisable for use in areas where gay people are a well-organized political force.

See also: *mine field*

fairness
Often nothing could be more obvious or more platitudinous.

"Democrats agree that America needs a trade policy based on the simple premise of *fairness.*" (Senator Lloyd M. Bentsen, July 21, 1988)

faith
A proper attitude of reverence and respect, channeled in appropriate directions.

"On every continent and in every land to which Mrs. Johnson and I traveled, we found *faith* and hope and love toward this land of America and toward our people." (Lyndon B. Johnson, January 8, 1964)

"The real fire within the builders of America was *faith—faith* in a Provident God whose hand supported and guided them; *faith* in themselves as the children of God . . . *faith* in their country and its principles that proclaimed man's right to freedom and justice." (Dwight D. Eisenhower, May 4, 1952)

faith, deep and abiding
The best kind of faith; much better than shallow and transitory.

". . . with the memory in my heart of the young man, who arrived at Ellis Island with only $25 in his pocket, but with a *deep and abiding faith* in the promise of America." (Michael Dukakis, July 21, 1988)

faith, man of

USAGE: Toss in this accolade especially when you want to draw a contrast to antagonists who lack appropriate religiosity.

"Despite the chaos, despite the universal doubts, a determined band of patriotic Vietnamese around one *man of faith,* President Diem, began to release and to harness the latent power of nationalism to create an independent, anti-Communist Vietnam." (John F. Kennedy, 1960)

Occasionally: woman of faith

See also: *Judeo-Christian*

faith in America

Woe be unto any national politician who doesn't proclaim its ever-deepening wonders.

"I have never had more *faith in America* than I do today." (Jimmy Carter, July 15, 1976)

false notions of equality

USAGE: If you think some people are getting carried away with egalitarian zeal, you might want to lob this one at them.

"Their mistaken course stems from *false notions of equality.* Equality rightly understood, as our Founding Fathers understood it, leads to liberty and to the emancipation of creative differences. Wrongly understood, as it has been so tragically in our time, it leads first to conformity and then to despotism." (Barry Goldwater, 1964)

See also: *color-conscious; quotas*

families, dysfunctional

For political purposes, a tightly circumscribed subset of the families that are actually dysfunctional; assumed to be primarily a problem among poor families.

USAGE: You should not publicly refer to "dysfunctional families" in the sense that the term is used in current psychological literature. While many analysts claim that the overwhelming majority of American families are severely "dysfunctional" in basic dynamics of communication and emotional clarity, you should not acknowledge that you have any inkling this might be the case. You must not disrupt the overall adulation of "the American family." If you wish to refer to "dysfunctional families," carefully limit the meaning with an evident assumption that such problems are largely confined to poor families. Most white voters will also get a message that you're not talking about white families. You certainly don't stand to gain if you seem to be informing or reminding most voters that their home life is not anywhere near what it's publicly cracked up to be.

"Take the biggest problem we've got in our country today. All these little children, millions of them, being robbed of their childhoods. Born into totally *dysfunctional families,* subjected at early ages to drug abuse, physical abuse, Lord only knows what else. Now, what's the answer at their level? Do they need family values like the conservatives say or more money spent on nutrition and health care programs. Well, with all deference, family values won't feed a hungry child but it sure is hard to raise that child without them." (Arkansas governor Bill Clinton, May 18, 1991)

Antonym: *American family, the*
See also: *pathology, tangle of*

family
An idealized social unit, existing in myth as a kind of miniature heaven; often experienced as a mishmash of blunted affections and honed cruelties. In political argot, idealization of family is a constant refrain, whereas negative realities are mentioned superficially and briefly if at all.

USAGE: In your repertoire of paeans, keep the familial theme high on the list. Many people treasure the idea of family, even if they aren't too crazy about their own.

"The *family* is the cornerstone of our society." (Lyndon B. Johnson, June 4, 1965)

"The *family* is the cornerstone of American life." (Jimmy Carter, October 4, 1976)

"A *family* does not ignore the sickness or pain of any of its children. A *family* gives all its members help and love. That's the kind of *families* we have, and that's the kind of Nation we want." (Jimmy Carter, July 18, 1988)

"*Families* are the bedrock of our nation—teachers of co-operation, tolerance, concern, and responsibility." (Ronald Reagan, February 9, 1982)

See also: *American family, the; pro-family; values, family*

family breakdown
USAGE: By likening the family unit to a stalled engine, you can make the solutions sound mechanical and straightforward rather than complicated and introspective.

"The evidence of *family breakdown* is all around us." (Jimmy Carter, October 4, 1976)

"In the welfare culture, the *breakdown of the family,* the most basic support system, has reached crisis proportions—in female and child poverty, child abandonment, horrible crimes and deteriorating schools." (Ronald Reagan, February 6, 1986)

See also: *family; moral erosion*

fanatics

People with strong views that are unpopular in U.S. society. USAGE: May be applied to foreigners who express confrontational nationalism with their actions (e.g., burning an American flag). Must never be applied to American troops whose bombs burn flags and people in other countries.

"Often the American flag's unique power to move and inspire is only evident when displayed in times of crisis. Like . . . on the day it was burned by chanting Iranian *fanatics* during the hostage crisis." (Senator Dan Coats, July 1989)

"The administration at first attempted to appease the homosexual rights *fanatics* by creating a special immigration waiver policy." (Senator Jesse Helms, January 14, 1991)

Synonym: *zealots*
Antonym: *patriots*

fascism

A label for totalitarianism sometimes loosely bandied about to the point of absurdity.

"*Fascism* was really the basis of the New Deal." (Ronald Reagan, 1976)

fashionable

Of course, it is always fashionable to pose as being steadfastly unconcerned with fashion.

"I know it may not be *fashionable* to speak of patriotism or national destiny these days, but I feel it is appropriate to do so on this occasion." (Richard M. Nixon, November 3, 1969)

"Economic loyalty to one's fellow countrymen is not a value that is *fashionable* in America today." (former senator Paul E. Tsongas, March 1991)

fat cats
See: *bigwigs*

fatally weaken this office
Make me look bad. Maybe even prove that I'm guilty of a crime.

"The Committee has the full story of Watergate, in so far as it relates to Presidential knowledge and Presidential actions. Production of these additional conversations would merely prolong the inquiry without yielding significant additional evidence. More fundamentally, continuing ad infinitum the process of yielding up additional conversations in response to an endless series of demands would *fatally weaken this office* not only in this Administration but for future Presidencies as well." (Richard M. Nixon, May 22, 1974)

See also: *massive invasion into the confidentiality of*

Father of our Country
USAGE: Homage to this guy is usually a safe bet. (However, see cautionary note below.)

"It is right that the memory of Washington be with us today, not only because this is our Bicentennial Inauguration, but because Washington remains the *Father of our Country*." (George Bush, January 20, 1989)

Caution: In strongly feminist or black precincts, such a reference to George Washington might meet with some resistance. Certain voters may take it amiss that there is no similar extolling of a "Mother of our Country," or may look askance at George Washington's place on a pedestal because he owned slaves.

feds, the
Slightly disapproving slang for the federal government and/
or federal officials.
USAGE: Conveys that you are irreverent toward federal authority and sympathize with constituents who view it as sus-
pect.

feeding frenzy
USAGE: When disclosures threaten your power, declare that
they are part of a "feeding frenzy." Evokes imagery of ag-
gressive journalists and opposition politicians as wacko pi-
ranha tearing innocent human flesh from bone.

first-strike weapons
USAGE: Never apply to U.S. nuclear weaponry.
     See also: *deterrence; modern weapons systems; moderniza-
tion; nuclear stockpile, total*

fiscal conservative
Frugal.

fiscal discipline
See: *austerity measures*

fiscally irresponsible
USAGE: For a budget you don't support.

fiscally responsible
USAGE: For a budget you do support.

flag, the
Always good for a high-profile and reverential pledge of
allegiance.
     "You Senators and reporters—you better saddle your

horses and put on your spurs if you're going to keep up with Johnson on *the flag,* mother and corruption." (Lyndon B. Johnson, March 5, 1956)

"We do not blindly follow traditions. But we do care deeply about symbols—particularly that one symbol of ideas and values for which men and women have sacrificed and died in every generation. To desecrate *the flag,* I believe, is to desecrate their memory and make light of their sacrifice." (Senator Dan Coats, July 1989)

Synonym: Old Glory

See also: *guaranteed respect*

flag-burners
See: *anti-American; fanatics*

fledgling democracies
Sometimes very ominous birds abroad, with distinct similarities to full-grown vultures. The label can be applied to countries where death squads are perched on a branch of government.

"I rise to express my strong support for the National Endowment for Democracy. . . . The withdrawal of endowment funds would mean the abandonment of *fledgling democracies* that depend on the endowment for assistance." (Representative Benjamin A. Gilman)

See also: *free and open democratic elections; friend of the United States; moderate; our allies*

flexibility
USAGE: Often a key word in an exhortation for expediency, which you'll want to package as principled pragmatism.

"We have to give Michael Dukakis the *flexibility* that this platform now provides." (Representative Edward Markey, July 19, 1988, urging the Democratic National Convention to reject a proposed pledge for no first use of nuclear weapons.)

flimflam

USAGE: A way you can refer to any deceptive fast talk that you don't find beneficial.

See also: *voodoo*

flip-flop

An opponent's change in position.

Antonyms: *modify my position; policy review*

forefathers

Foremothers need not apply.

"We should emulate the valor and the determination of our *forefathers*—those brave men who conquered the physical frontiers of this vast continent." (Harry S Truman, March 23, 1946)

"We are going to make America what our *forefathers* said it would be." (Gerald R. Ford, November 1, 1976)

"Our *forefathers* labored mightily to establish America as the preeminent economic power on earth." (former senator Paul E. Tsongas, March 1991)

See also: *America, the promise of; Founding Fathers*

forest for the trees, can't see the

USAGE: If opponents keep coming up with specific facts that run counter to your argument, you might try saying that they "can't see the forest for the trees."

See also: *bean counting*

forgotten stepchild

A metaphorical characterization that can make a multibillion-dollar industry sound more like an abandoned orphan.

"To the Administration, coal seems to have become nothing more than a poor, *forgotten stepchild*. It has become the stepchild who is briefly patted on the back but is given no allowance." (Senator Wendell H. Ford, March 19, 1991)

Founding Fathers
These fathers knew best.

"The *Founding Fathers* of our nation were wise and practical men, steeped in the traditions of democratic debate and hardened by the rigors of war. They understood . . ." (Senator Daniel K. Inouye, January 12, 1991)

"One hundred seventy-five years ago, the *founding fathers* of the American Republic declared . . ." (Dwight D. Eisenhower, July 3, 1951)

See also: *Valley Forge*

free and open democratic elections
Elections with desired results.

"Our policy consistently has been to bring peace and freedom to all of Central America. Today four of the five Central American countries choose their governments in *free and open democratic elections*." (Ronald Reagan, February 24, 1988, contending that the odd nation out was Nicaragua—which had held 1984 elections seen by international observers as far more fair than elections in El Salvador, a country with government-linked death squads.)

See also: *fledgling democracies*

free enterprise system
USAGE: Whatever your economic agenda, insist that the "free enterprise system" will benefit.

"Small business is key to the success of our *free enterprise system*." (Representative Richard Baker, May 8, 1991)

"The American *free enterprise system* is alive and well in Decatur, Texas." (Senator Phil Gramm, December 5, 1989)

"Taken together and placed in the context of our *free enterprise system,* these progressive actions made America the land of opportunity." (Senator Lloyd M. Bentsen, July 21, 1988)

"In this long and critical struggle, the American *system of free enterprise* must be our major weapon." (Robert F. Kennedy, August 1963)

"We want prosperity, and in a *free enterprise system* there can be no prosperity without profit. We want a growing economy, and there can be no growth without the investment that is inspired and financed by profit." (John F. Kennedy, April 30, 1962)

"The responsibility of preserving our *free enterprise system* will continue to rest upon the joint efforts of business, labor, the farmers, and the Government. There must be moderation on the part of business, forbearance on the part of labor, all-out effort on the part of the farmer, and wise guidance and action on the part of the Government." (Harry S Truman, April 21, 1947)

free-market principles
Economic structures, notions, procedures, and laws compatible with the desires of U.S.-based corporations.

"I praise our neighbors to the South for their commitment to these negotiations and particularly for the actions they have independently taken to develop a more open economy based on *free-market principles* and fair competition." (Representative Bill Archer, May 3, 1991)

"We have been heartened and encouraged by President Yeltsin's commitment to democratic values and *free-market principles,* and we look forward to working with him." (George Bush, June 20, 1991)

free markets
Economic setups advantageous to some. Often equated with a wide variety of freedoms that may or may not be related to "free markets."
USAGE: Lends itself to catchy alliteration when combined with other phrases also beginning with the word "free."

"We know how to secure a more just and prosperous life for man on Earth: through *free markets,* free speech, free elections, and the exercise of free will unhampered by the state." (George Bush, January 20, 1989)

See also: *free markets and free peoples; market economy*

free markets and free peoples
Has a good beat; American politicians and press can dance to it. The same can't be said of political prisoners inside numerous countries with "free markets."

free speech
USAGE: No matter how much you might want to limit it, keep proclaiming that you're for "free speech."

"I don't expect to muffle criticism. Every one of you say we invite *free speech* in our country and we want *free speech* and we want criticism—don't you? Every one of you do. But there is a limit to how much you want, and there is a ceiling on how much is good for you." (Lyndon B. Johnson, April 27, 1964)

"I propose the 'Federal Anti-Riot Act of 1968.' This new law will make it a felony, punishable by up to five years in prison, for any person to incite or organize a riot after having traveled in interstate commerce with the intention to do so. This is a narrow and carefully drawn bill. It does not impede *free speech* or peaceful assembly." (Lyndon B. Johnson, February 7, 1968)

"Ironically, on the 200th anniversary of our Bill of

Rights, we find *free speech* under assault throughout the United States. . . ." (George Bush, May 4, 1991)

See also: *political correctness; privilege*

free trade
Verbal commerce in ambiguity.
USAGE: If you say you favor "free trade," proceed to assume that it is defined however you choose.

"*Free trade* is both sensible economics and sane politics." (Lyndon B. Johnson, June 9, 1965)

free world
Rigidly proclaimed, the binary division of the globe into "free" and unfree zones tends to be simplistic gobbledygook.
USAGE: Never hurts.

"The *free world* has one great factor in common. We are not held together by force, but we are held together by this great factor. . . . The *free world* believes, under one religion or another, in a Divine Power, it believes in a Supreme Being." (Dwight D. Eisenhower, July 15, 1955)

"This nation, this government, this administration have no foes in the capitals of the *free world.*" (Lyndon B. Johnson, June 9, 1965)

"I want America to again become the hope and beacon of a *free world,* jealously guarding human rights for all human beings and the right to self-determination." (Jesse Jackson, November 3, 1983)

"Now, in contrast, the greatest Nation of the *free world* has had a leader for eight straight years that has pretended that he cannot hear our questions over the noise of the helicopter." (Texas State treasurer Ann W. Richards, July 18, 1988)

freedom

A word with the potential for enormous meaning and vibrant immediacy. But served up by uncounted politicians
(and ad copywriters), "freedom" is a rhetorical staple,
more warmed over than those canned string beans in the
school cafeteria.

"We are indisputably the world's most powerful force for
freedom and economic growth." (George Bush, June 12,
1991)

"Of all the blessings of our Nation, *freedom* is surely the
most precious." (Lyndon B. Johnson, July 4, 1967)

"We stand for *freedom.* That is our conviction for ourselves; that is our only commitment to others." (John F.
Kennedy, May 25, 1961)

"*Freedom* has never been an abstract idea to us here in
the United States. It is real and concrete." (Harry S Truman, November 6, 1950)

freedom fighters

Any favored insurgent army, no matter how cruel its actions or despotic its orientation.

"The *freedom fighters* of Afghanistan would tell us as well
that the threat of aggression has not receded from the
world." (Ronald Reagan, June 9, 1982)

"If Congress doesn't vote support for the Nicaraguan
freedom fighters soon, we are looking at an irreversible surrender to the forces of communism. . . ." (George Bush,
July 20, 1988)

freedom for the police

An odd concept. But since any number of advertisements
routinely link consumer products to "freedom," the rhetorical notion of "freedom for the police" may stand as good a
chance of going over big as a shiny new-model Chevrolet.

"*Freedom for the police* is denied when their resources are unduly limited." (Virginia governor L. Douglas Wilder, January 13, 1990)

freeloaders
Those who take advantage of the resources of others. Rarely applied to wealthy individuals and corporations with lucrative activities subsidized by government largess.

"Unemployment insurance is a prepaid vacation plan for *freeloaders*." (Ronald Reagan)

fresh approach
See: *renewal*

friend of the United States
An ally that won't step out of line.

"To further emphasize the fact that a new South African Government completely dominated by the ANC will not be a *friend of the United States,* I would also call attention to the January 19, 1991, statement by the ANC itself with regard to the war in the Persian Gulf. . . . [A]ny government dominated by it, is not, and will not be, a *friend of the United States.*" (Senator Jesse Helms, February 26, 1991)

"The President of Mexico is a *friend of the United States,* and his relationship with President Bush bodes well for both our countries." (Representative Duncan Hunter, April 15, 1991)

friends
Among politicians, this term can be spoken through clenched teeth, meaning that they are not at each other's throats today. More generally, a common noun of politeness without substance.

"We came here as *friends* and so you will find very little

grist for the mill that this is a personal feud." (Senator Charles S. Robb, June 18, 1991)

"We want people to know that we are *friends*." (Virginia governor L. Douglas Wilder, June 18, 1991)

"Our *friends* in the environmental community may be disappointed that we haven't gone far enough. But, based on what is known today, I think this bill goes as far as we can." (Senator Quentin N. Burdick, April 25, 1991)

Antonym: cronies
See also: *my good friend*

frontier
USAGE: Has an all-American intrepid westward-ho sound to it.

"We must achieve and pioneer in the great *frontier* of human rights and social justice." (Harry S Truman, October 13, 1948)

"The New *Frontier*" (John F. Kennedy)

"America, our beautiful America, is the land of the perpetual *frontier*." (Lyndon B. Johnson, October 8, 1964)

"Our party was built out of the sweatshops of the old Lower East Side, the dark mills of New Hampshire, the blazing hearths of Illinois, the coal mines of Pennsylvania, the hard-scrabble farms of the southern coastal plains, and the unlimited *frontiers* of America." (Jimmy Carter, July 15, 1976)

"It's time to meet the challenge of the next American *frontier,* the challenge of building an economic future for our country. . . ." (Michael Dukakis, July 21, 1988)

See also: *manifest destiny*

full picture
All the information.
USAGE: When you agree with the president on a foreign

policy issue, you can assert that nobody else really knows the complete truth—kind of like a TV show that might be called *President Knows Best.* (Any resemblance between the chief executive and Robert Young as Jim Anderson can only help.) For good measure you might imply that members of Congress are neophyte adults compared to the omniscient paternal presidency.

"It is my belief that the President, with all the assets of statecraft and updated intelligence at his disposal, is uniquely positioned to make that judgment. Only he has the *full picture.* . . . Even with the best of intentions, the U.S. Congress is simply ill-equipped to perform a similar function." (Senator Warren B. Rudman, January 12, 1991)

future, the
USAGE: Should be high on your mantra list.

"Let us always, even as we rightly revere the past and its heritage of freedom, never fear or doubt *the future.* For this —*the future*—is the hope and the home of all who are young and are free—if they are but brave." (Dwight D. Eisenhower, June 11, 1953)

"We face a clear-cut choice this year between the past and *the future,* between more of the same and a new beginning." (Jimmy Carter, October 19, 1976)

"This is a strong commitment to space, to science and to *the future* and this is obviously good news for Texas and America." (Senator Phil Gramm, February 7, 1989, speaking of supercollider and space-station budget items.)

"We believe we ought to have a federal budget which spends more money on *the future* and less on the present and the past." (Arkansas governor Bill Clinton, May 6, 1991)

future, hope for the
USAGE: Should spring eternal from podiums, since most people prefer to hear optimistic prattle instead of realistic assessments.

"As a private citizen, Ed Muskie has continued to give our country counsel, confidence, continuity. As a Democrat, he has proven that we stand for economic growth, for equality of opportunity, and *hope for the future.*" (Senator Brock Adams, July 18, 1988)

Antonym: doom and gloom
See also: *optimist*

Gg Hh

"G" is for God Bless You
"H" is for Human Rights

Georgetown-Manhattan-Hyannisport elitist axis
"My last talk down here discombobulated the whole *Georgetown-Manhattan-Hyannisport elitist axis.* Let's see what this one does." (Spiro Agnew, October 28, 1970)

get it right
A phrase that sounds pithy enough so that people may not notice how presumptuous and shallow it is.
USAGE: Hopefully you won't be pressed to go into any depth about what "it" is.

"I shudder to think of the consequences if we do not *get it right* this time—but I have to be honest. I have my doubts. I wonder if we are serious enough about energy to solve the problem at long last." (Representative John D. Dingell, February 26, 1991)

"After years of weapons systems that wouldn't work, cost overruns, and corporate fraud, a lack of confidence in our equipment was understandable. But Desert Storm proved we could *get it right*." (Representative Jolene Unsoeld, March 8, 1991)

getting our arms around
Administrative lingo to convey the idea that things are under control.

"We are *getting our arms around* the problems." (Secretary of Energy James D. Watkins, June 1991)

giveaway at taxpayers' expense
Frugal bombast.
USAGE: A nice fit for any number of press releases, talk shows, etc.

God
Undefinable.
USAGE: An old standby.

"And a country then was created by men and women who came not for gold but mainly in search of *God*. . . . Do we really think that we can have it both ways, that *God* will protect us in a time of crisis even as we turn away from him in our day-to-day life? It's time to realize, I think, that we need *God* more than he needs us. But millions of Americans haven't forgotten." (Ronald Reagan, February 9, 1982)

". . . let us go forward, firm in our faith, steadfast in our purpose, cautious of the dangers; but sustained by our confidence in the will of *God* and the promise of man." (Richard M. Nixon, January 20, 1969)

"No man who enters the office to which I have succeeded can fail to recognize how every President of the United States has placed special reliance on his faith in *God*." (John F. Kennedy, February 9, 1961)

"Without *God* there could be no American form of government, nor an American way of life. Recognition of the Supreme Being is the first—the most basic—expression of Americanism. Thus the founding fathers of America saw it, and thus, with *God*'s help, it will continue to be." (Dwight D. Eisenhower, February 27, 1955)

"America is the greatest force that *God* has ever allowed to exist on His footstool." (Dwight D. Eisenhower, April 5, 1954)

"When the United States was established, its coins bore witness to the American faith in a benevolent deity. The motto then was 'In *God* We Trust.' That is still our motto and we, as a people, still place our firm trust in *God*." (Harry S Truman, October 30, 1949)

"I walked the floor of the White House night after night until midnight, and I am not ashamed to tell you, gentlemen, that I went down on my knees and prayed Almighty *God* for light and guidance more than one night. And one night late it came to me this way—I don't know how it was but it came. . . . That there was nothing left for us to do but to take them all, and to educate the Filipinos, and uplift and civilize and Christianize them, and by *God*'s grace do the very best we could by them as our fellowmen for whom Christ also died. And then I went to bed and went to sleep, and slept soundly, and the next morning I sent for the chief engineer of the War Department (our map-maker), and I told him to put the Philippines on the map of the United States." (William McKinley, 1898)

See also: *sleepless nights; under God*

God bless you

USAGE: A righteous way to close a speech. Not to be confused with *Gesundheit*.

"*God bless you,* and thank you." (Ronald Reagan, January 20, 1981)

"Thank you, and *God bless you.*" (Ronald Reagan, February 9, 1982)

"*God bless you* and may God bless America." (Ronald Reagan, January 21, 1985)

"Thank you and welcome to Atlanta! And *God bless you.* Atlanta loves you. America loves you. . . . *God bless you* and thank you for coming to Atlanta." (Atlanta mayor Andrew Young, July 18, 1988)

"Thank you. *God bless you.* Good night. On to victory! Thank you." (Jimmy Carter, July 18, 1988)

"And so, good-bye, *God bless you,* and God bless the United States of America." (Ronald Reagan, January 11, 1989)

"Thank you. *God bless you* and God bless the United States of America." (George Bush, January 20, 1989)

"Thank you very much, and *God bless you.*" (Arkansas governor Bill Clinton, June 15, 1991)

See also: *America, God bless the United States of; under God*

God-fearing

Implicitly, knowing who's really boss. More generally, deferential to duly constituted authority (i.e., demigod-fearing).

"The true image of Washington is not that of power or pomp or plenty. It is, rather, that of a prayerful capital of good and *God-fearing* people." (Lyndon B. Johnson, February 5, 1964)

"As a result of the growing power of Washington, we

have already become a government-fearing people instead
of a *God-fearing* people." (George Wallace, 1972)

"So I tell you there are a great many *God-fearing*, dedicated, noble men and women in public life, present company included." (Ronald Reagan, March 8, 1983)

Antonym: *atheists*

God's help
USAGE: You may as well solicit it in key speeches. Do not do
so, though, if you are a minor officeholder; it might seem
presumptuous to voice a request for "God's help" if you're
a county assessor or something like that.

"Today, I ask your prayers that in the years ahead I may
have *God's help* in making decisions that are right for
America. . . ." (Richard M. Nixon, January 20, 1973)

"The crisis we are facing today . . . does require, however, our best effort, and our willingness to believe in ourselves and to believe in our capacity to perform great
deeds; to believe that together, with *God's help,* we can and
will resolve the problems which now confront us." (Ronald
Reagan, January 20, 1981)

See also: *so help me God*

good
An adjective that offers people reassurances of essential
virtue, a kind of happy-face sticker to obscure dire social
dynamics.

"I know America. I know the heart of America is *good.*"
(Richard M. Nixon, January 20, 1969)

Americans are "a *good* people." (Richard M. Nixon, repeatedly during his presidency)

"If we can just have a government—as I've said a thousand times—as *good* as our people are, that's all we could

hope for and that's all we could expect and that's enough."
(Jimmy Carter, November 3, 1976)

A Government As Good As Its People (title of a book by
Jimmy Carter, 1977)

"Americans are a caring people. We are a *good* people, a
generous people." (George Bush, March 6, 1991)

good-faith effort
USAGE: When it's under your aegis, every effort is "good-
faith," no matter how unsuccessful (or disingenuous).
When made by a properly demonized foreigner, no effort
can be.

good will begets good will
If they scratch my back, I'll scratch theirs.
USAGE: A good way to bridge the dilemma of needing to
encourage tacit deals with hostile foreign governments
while also needing to claim that you aren't about to make
any deals with them.

"There are today Americans who are held against their
will in foreign lands, and Americans who are unaccounted
for. Assistance can be shown here, and will be long remembered. *Good will begets good will.* Good faith can be a spiral
that endlessly moves on." (George Bush, January 20, 1989)

govern
Often a high-blown verb for protecting certain interests at
the expense of others.

"The people who own the country ought to *govern* it."
(John Jay, Continental Congress president and first U.S.
Supreme Court chief justice)

"In a free society, those with the power to *govern* are
necessarily responsive to those with the right to vote."
(John F. Kennedy, February 28, 1963)

"Let's resolve that in this Convention we're going to show to the American people the picture of a Party that has its act together and is ready to *govern.*" (House Speaker Jim Wright, July 18, 1988)

govern by symbols

USAGE: When the other party is successful at dominating governmental decisions, you might find this catchphrase helpful for concocting an alibi to deflect attention from the ineffectual response of your own party.

"Bush can deflect controversy and *govern by symbols* because he does not have an agenda." (Representative David Obey, June 1991)

See also: *loyal opposition*

government interference

Disliked governmental actions.

Gramm-Rudman

USAGE: If you want eyes to glaze over, talk about Gramm-Rudman budgetary provisions for a few minutes. Hopefully your listeners will be suitably impressed that you seem to know what you're talking about, and so bored that they won't try to find out for sure.

See also: *debt ceiling*

great

Perhaps the most abused and overused adjective of oratorical puffery.

"Nobody in this world can put on a political rally like that *great* executive Dick Daley of Chicago. He makes it so much fun being a Democrat that you don't see how anybody could be anything else." (Lyndon B. Johnson, October 30, 1964)

"Norman Mineta . . . is a highly respected member of Congress for the last 14 years. And Norman is a leading expert on federal budget matters, and ladies and gentlemen, a *great* American." (Representative Esteban E. Torres, July 18, 1988)

"And now it is my privilege and pleasure to yield to the *great* Congressman from the State of Texas, Martin Frost." (Democratic National Convention Rules Committee chair Kathleen M. Vick, July 18, 1988)

"Let it be very clear that when the *great* Mayor of the *great* city of Washington, D.C., Marion Barry, and a United States Senator from Louisiana could both come and recommend unanimously the rules for this 1988 Convention, I can assure you that it is a good and a solid set of rules to guide our Convention." (Senator John Breaux, July 18, 1988)

". . . the *great* Speaker of the House of Representatives, our Permanent Chair of this Convention, let's hear it for the Congressman from Texas, the Speaker, Jim Wright." (Democratic National Committee chair Paul G. Kirk, Jr., July 18, 1988)

". . . a man who won friends little by little, until finally, he was gaining *great* momentum as a candidate for the Presidential nomination, who has made *great* contributions as a governor of one of our *great* states and who still has many *great* contributions to make to the Democratic Party and the United States, former Governor Bruce Babbitt of Arizona." (House Speaker Jim Wright, July 18, 1988)

"Clinton looked good . . . everyone is telling me it was a *great* speech." (Representative Bill Richardson, July 20, 1988)

"This is not a success produced by one fellow in Washington. But rather, a success achieved by a *great* company in a *great* town with *great* workers who can compete with any workers in the world." (Senator Phil Gramm, September 18, 1988)

See also: *dynamic; terrific*

great adventure
"This is our *great adventure,* and a wonderful one it is." (Hubert H. Humphrey, on a vice presidential visit to Saigon, speaking about the Vietnam War to U.S. embassy staff.)

great day for America
Don't bet on it.

"This is a *great day for America* and a bad day for the Communists." (Senator Joseph R. McCarthy, October 19, 1951)

"Mr. Speaker, members of Congress, and distinguished guests, it is a great day to be a soldier, and it is a *great day to be an American.*" (General Norman Schwarzkopf, May 8, 1991)

great experiment
Sometimes known as "democracy."

Great Society
Obsolete.

A raisin in the sun, long since burned to a crisp.

"So I ask you tonight to join me and march along the road to the future, the road that leads to the *Great Society,* where no child will go unfed and no youngster will go unschooled; where every child has a good teacher and every teacher has good pay, and both have good classrooms; where every human being has dignity and every worker has a job; where education is blind to color and employment is unaware of race; where decency prevails and courage abounds." (Lyndon B. Johnson, May 28, 1964)

"We will have our *Great Society* one day. And when it's finished we'll have a society where there is a joy of living, a life of purpose. A society young of spirit and young of heart, but mature in mind. A society with love of children, and with respect for its elders. A society which works for education and strives for human dignity. A society where everyone—black, white, young, old, man, woman—EVERYONE is important. A society where culture and beauty are a main course and not a dessert. A society where everyone is productive and a full participant in American life." (Hubert H. Humphrey, April 18, 1966)

See also: *war on poverty*

greatest country

A pandering punch line for just about any stem-winder.
USAGE: You can alternate nearly a dozen permutations by combining "greatest country" or "greatest nation" with "on earth," "on the planet," "in the world," "in history," or "ever known"; maybe you can think of others. Just remember to take this snippet out of your boilerplate script when you're overseas speaking to foreigners.

"We, too, can be just as tough, just as realistic, just as hard bargainers as Mr. Khrushchev. And we can win. For this is still the *greatest country* on earth." (John F. Kennedy, October 1, 1959)

". . . we still live in the *greatest* and the strongest and the best *country* on earth." (Jimmy Carter, September 23, 1976)

"It is outrageous that the *greatest nation* in the world has no better control over its own spending." (Representative Wayne Allard, May 1991)

"We live in the *greatest country* in the world, but I believe our priorities are misplaced." (Representative Jolene Unsoeld, June 7, 1991)

See also: *number one; superpower, only; unbeatable*

greatness
Always the destiny of the United States. Anyone inclined to argue the point is not destined for electoral greatness.
USAGE: Can be effectively linked with rightness and myriad other virtues.

"Our *greatness* as a nation has been our capacity to do what has to be done when we knew our course was right." (Richard M. Nixon, November 3, 1969)

". . . to lead our party back to victory and our nation back to *greatness*. . . . Ours is the party of a brave young President who called the young at heart, regardless of age, to seek a 'New Frontier' of national *greatness*—John F. Kennedy." (Jimmy Carter, July 15, 1976)

"I've come more and more to appreciate the diversity and the *greatness* of our country since I have been a candidate for President." (Jimmy Carter, October 4, 1976)

"My fellow citizens, our Nation is poised for *greatness*. We must do what we know is right and do it with all our might." (Ronald Reagan, January 21, 1985)

"Yes, my friends, it's a time for wonderful new beginnings: a little baby, a new administration, a new era of *greatness* for America." (Michael Dukakis, July 21, 1988)

"Mr. Speaker, America and the world are today very proud of the military which has achieved a victory unparalleled in the course of modern history. The bravery and professionalism of our soldiers, sailors, airmen, and marines and the brilliant leadership and planning of Generals Powell and Schwarzkopf and our other military commanders are living testimony to the *greatness* of America and our democratic system." (Representative Charles W. Stenholm, March 5, 1991)

"America's *greatness* is under attack." (former senator Paul E. Tsongas, 1991; the opening sentence of an eighty-six-page position paper for his presidential campaign. The second page of the document begins: "America is *greatness.*")

greenies
USAGE: Denouncing "reds" is passé, but "greenies" can be blasted as dangerous tree-huggers bent on fiendish schemes.

"The *greenies* have led us into the crisis in the Middle East. . . . The rabid environmentalists felt it was more important to jeopardize the lives of our brave American servicemen than risk the death of a single snail darter." (Representative Tom DeLay, November 3, 1990)

guaranteed
Traditionally a dubious guarantee.

"I suggest the propriety of setting apart an ample district west of the Mississippi . . . to be *guaranteed* to the Indian tribes, as long as they shall occupy it." (Andrew Jackson, 1829, presidential message to Congress)

guaranteed respect
An oxymoron to the effect that people can be forced to feel what can only be engendered or earned.

"The American flag must be *guaranteed respect*—even if that takes a constitutional amendment." (Senator Dan Coats, October 1989)

handwringing
Failing to be decisive and (implicitly) macho enough.

"Indeed, it would be the supreme irony if this body, after so much *handwringing* over the prospect of hostilities, were unwilling or incapable of making this fateful choice. I submit that neither history nor the American people would soon forgive such an abdication of will." (Senator Warren B. Rudman, January 12, 1991)

Antonyms: *bite the bullet; bold; leadership*
See also: *impotent; wimp*

hard choices
USAGE: Your choices.

"I know how difficult the choices are: I have had to make them all to put this budget together. Those *hard choices* cannot be evaded, and trying to duck them will only make our difficult problem worse." (New York governor Mario M. Cuomo, February 13, 1991)

See also: *tough choices*

hardball politics
A figure of speech that can make complaints about political chicanery seem like they're coming from naive persons with overly thin cowhide.

"It was just good old *hardball* American *politics.*" (Virginia Republican Legislative Caucus director Steve Haner, June 20, 1991)

See also: *rough-and-tumble*

hard-earned
USAGE: The best way to describe money that the government gets from taxpayers, when you want to gain a bit more momentum by channeling resentment for your own purposes.

"Mr. Speaker, the American people are scandalized by the HUD scam and the S&L debacle which have wasted billions of their *hard-earned* dollars." (Representative Tom Campbell, January 28, 1991)

"The American people have the right to know how their *hard-earned* tax dollars are being spent, and if they are being spent efficiently." (Representative Henry B. Gonzalez, July 27, 1990)

See also: *taxpayers*

hard-line
Antonym: firm

hate war
USAGE: Especially handy when you want to calm fears of war. The more you expect war, the more you should be heard proclaiming how much you detest it; that way, when war comes, hopefully you won't get blamed.

"I have seen war. . . . I *hate war*." (Franklin D. Roosevelt, August 14, 1936)

"I *hate war*. And if the day ever comes when my vote must be cast to send your boy to the trenches, that day Lyndon Johnson will leave his Senate seat to go with him." (Lyndon B. Johnson, 1941)

"We love peace. We *hate war*. But our course is charted always by the compass of honor." (Lyndon B. Johnson, April 10, 1965)

"And I *hate war*. Love peace. And we have peace. And I am not going to let anyone take it away from us." (George Bush, August 18, 1988)

See also: *assurance*

heal

USAGE: A good verb for encouraging people to think of you as a kind of Marcus Welby, M.D., for the body politic.

"I want to help bring about the changes that will *heal* America and lead us to new victories." (George Wallace, 1972)

"I believe that we have lived through a time of torment, and now we are near a time of *healing*—if the people rule again. I ask you to help us reach that point of *healing,* to help us bind up our nation's wounds." (Jimmy Carter, October 4, 1976, speaking to the National Conference of Catholic Charities.)

"For myself and for our nation I want to thank my predecessor for all he has done to *heal* our land." (Jimmy Carter, January 20, 1977)

"The best accomplishment was the *healing* of the American people and the change in attitude toward their government. People have forgotten how distrustful the American people were of their government in Washington because of Watergate, Vietnam. We remember those riots on college campuses and in many of our metropolitan areas. Families were torn apart. It was a very unpleasant period in American history and I think my administration *healed* those differences." (Gerald R. Ford, November 28, 1987)

"Leaders must build; leaders must *heal.*" (Jesse Jackson, July 15, 1988)

Caution: In written statements, do not confuse with "heel." A slipup could prove embarrassing.

heartfelt love

When used in the third person to describe someone else's emotions, a shamelessly fraudulent claim to know what is in another's heart.

"Leadership is another key ingredient of success, and

Generals Powell and Schwarzkopf exemplified true leadership. They provided a clear, long-term vision for the campaign and a brilliant strategy to achieve the objective—and yet these battle-hardened men displayed a *heartfelt love* and concern for the rank-and-file that moved them close to tears during public briefings." (Representative Jolene Unsoeld, March 8, 1991)

See also: *caring; compassion*

herd journalism
USAGE: An effective put-down of reporters, as long as no one is around to point out the similarities with herd politics.

heritage
USAGE: Expressing pride in one's ancestry and upbringing is *de rigueur,* of course. But this may be a bit sticky if your family tree has golden roots. Enormous wealth is not to be flaunted in the political arena, all the less so if it has been yours since birth; in that case, try to present the silver spoon as just another "heritage."

"Well, one thing that you know is that we have a very proud family and a wonderful *heritage.* And I'm not going to change that name, because I am proud of it. Secondly, it doesn't really make any difference. Growing up in my hometown, I was like any other skinny little kid who wasn't very good at baseball, and wasn't much turned on by arithmetic in school. I don't think I was different from anyone else." (Pierre S. du Pont IV, January 16, 1988)

heritage, American
Of course there are many "American heritages," ranging from glorious and admirable to cruel and despicable. When

politicians exult in "American heritage," their adulation is selective indeed.

heroes
Even inanimate objects can qualify, especially if lethal.

"The F-117, with its precision-guided munitions, was one of the *heroes* of the Persian Gulf." (Representative Les Aspin, June 20, 1991)

higher motivation
USAGE: A marvelous thing to tell poor people to seek.

highrollers
See: *bigwigs*

hire by the numbers
Ensure equal opportunity in practice and not just in theory.

"The bill's presumption of guilt and high hurdle of proof will force employers to *hire by the numbers.*" (Representative Henry J. Hyde, June 4, 1991)

See also: *quotas*

historical basis
Any similarity to actual history is apt to be intermittent at best.

"From an *historical basis,* Middle East conflicts do not last a long time." (Dan Quayle, October 2, 1990)

history teaches that
Fill in the blank.

USAGE: A preamble for whatever aphorism suits your occasion.

"*History teaches that* wars begin when governments believe the price of aggression is cheap." (Ronald Reagan, January 16, 1984)

"But what does recent *history* teach us about the effectiveness of sanctions in averting conflicts and stopping injustice? It *teaches* us, Mr. President, *that* embargoes can postpone a tyrant's ability to realize his goals, but not his will to ultimately secure them." (Senator John Seymour, January 12, 1991)

homegrown
Acceptable to us.

". . . we've also spoken to the Palestinian leadership, because there is every evidence that these riots are not just spontaneous and *homegrown*." (Ronald Reagan, February 24, 1988)

homegrown resource
USAGE: Makes whatever you're talking about sound at least a little bit more down-home and all-American.

"These facts show that coal will continue to be a major part of the energy supply mix for many years to come. It simply will not make sense to stop using this *homegrown* resource. The recent war in the Persian Gulf should be enough to remind us of the need for products made in the U.S.A." (Senator Wendell H. Ford, March 19, 1991)

honor and integrity
USAGE: It wouldn't do to say that you are jockeying for political advantage or trying to put the kibosh on an incipient scandal, so you might want to don the mantle of defender of a maligned public servant.

"We've got a man's *honor and integrity* on the line here." (George Bush, July 12, 1991, speaking of his nominee to head the CIA, Robert Gates.)

hope

USAGE: It should thump eternally and loudly in your breast. Remember, if you can't sugarcoat the situation then you're in the wrong profession.

"I am proud to be a member of a party that may have turned off the lights in the White House—but had turned on the lights of *hope* all across the land." (Lyndon B. Johnson, May 9, 1964)

hope, apostle of

"Michael Dukakis doesn't believe that for a minute. . . . He is an *apostle of hope*." (Arkansas governor Bill Clinton, July 20, 1988)

Antonyms: *doomsayers; naysayers; prophets of doom*

hope, the party of

The one you belong to, of course.

"We have always been *the party of hope*." (Senator Edward M. Kennedy, August 12, 1980)

hordes

Soldiers not quite human. Good candidates for being slaughtered with equanimity.

". . . with *hordes* of Chinese Communist troops poised just across the border. . . ." (John F. Kennedy, April 6, 1954)

See also: *attrit; casualties*

hostages

Some hostages are mentioned frequently, others not at all; depends on the politics of the captors and the nationalities of the captives.

See also: *terrorists*

housing, affordable
For many people, mythical housing.

human resources
Makes human beings sound like unmined ore.

". . . while economic growth certainly requires capital, it also requires other essential ingredients. . . . And most of all, it requires *human resources*—work force. Healthy, educated, skilled, motivated human beings." (New York governor Mario M. Cuomo, August 9, 1991)

human rights
Civil liberties in other countries.
USAGE: Although the United Nations' Universal Declaration of Human Rights includes references to food, housing, and medical care, your references to "human rights" abroad should exclude these categories so you won't conflict with the more limited civil-liberties definition accepted by U.S. mass media and government officials. Moreover, convention requires that in debates on U.S. domestic policies you not discuss even civil liberties issues as "human rights" issues. At the same time, you may as well claim that the United States has always been dedicated to "human rights"; though such a statement is hardly accurate, political protocol will shield you from criticism.

"The world itself is now dominated by a new spirit. People more numerous and more politically aware are craving and now demanding their place in the sun—not just for the benefit of their own physical condition, but for basic *human rights.*" (Jimmy Carter, January 20, 1977)

"Let the word go forth from this time and place, to friend and foe alike, that the torch has been passed to a new generation of Americans . . . unwilling to witness or permit the slow undoing of those *human rights* to which this nation has always been committed, and to which we are committed today at home and around the world." (John F. Kennedy, January 20, 1961)

"The United States has always had a deep concern for *human rights*. Religious freedom, free speech, and freedom of thought are cherished realities in our land." (Harry S Truman, January 7, 1948)

hypocrisy
Tilt!

Ii Jj

"I" is for Improprieties
"J" is for Just and Lasting Peace

I do not mean to imply
People didn't hear what they may have thought they just heard.
USAGE: A good verbal stratagem for when you've just implied something but don't want to get zinged for it.

"*I do not mean to imply* that protection of the environment is not important. It is very important. However . . ." (Senator Wendell H. Ford, September 8, 1989)

I have a dream
Canned hope, often kept on a shelf and once in a while put on display.
USAGE: Whatever your views, repeating a phrase or two from Martin Luther King, Jr., can be advisable on occasion.

After all, he's not around to make trouble for politicians like you.

Derivation: The speech by King at the March on Washington for Jobs and Freedom, August 28, 1963.

ideologues

People whose political beliefs differ substantially from the beliefs of the person using this pejorative.

USAGE: This handy noun enables you to assert implicitly that while your target has an "ideology," you are above having any such thing. Works best if you're an adherent of centrist, status quo ideology that blends in with the prevailing scenery so you can easily claim to be reassuringly normal and without an ideological slant.

"And I must say that in the past eight years we have seen that good solid Republican *ideologues* can be just as wasteful and incompetent and fuzzy-headed as anyone who has ever lived." (Jimmy Carter, October 14, 1976)

"These archaic old saws are much embraced by party chieftains. The affection for them expressed by party *ideologues* is matched only by our trading competitors' fervent hope that they will never disappear." (former senator Paul E. Tsongas, March 1991)

ideology

Some other people's ideology.

"You know, national Democrats used to fight for the working families of America, and now all they seem to fight for are the special interests and their own left-wing *ideology*." (Ronald Reagan, October 26, 1984)

"We Democrats don't march in lockstep behind some narrow, rigid *ideology* of indifference. We are not gray grains of oatmeal in a bland porridge of privilege." (Senator Lloyd M. Bentsen, July 21, 1988)

See also: *orthodoxies, stale*

idleness

A somewhat dated word for an ethnic or cultural group's failure to do what the politician desires.

"The Utes are actual, practical Communists and the government should be ashamed to foster and encourage them in their *idleness* and wanton waste of property." (Denver politician William B. Vickers, 1879, writing about Rocky Mountain Indians in the *Denver Tribune*. At the time Vickers was secretary to Colorado governor Frederick W. Pitkin.)

ill-

A prefix with many uses, not the least of which is its alliterative possibilities.

USAGE: Sounds polite but can at least faintly imply that the opposition may be sick.

"Our conferees have consistently gone to the international bargaining table *ill*-staffed, *ill*-prepared and *ill*-advised." (John F. Kennedy, June 14, 1960)

I'm not a crook

USAGE: If things have deteriorated to the extent that these words come out of your mouth, you're probably in trouble. Retain a top-of-the-line PR firm. And a terrific lawyer.

"I welcome this kind of examination because people have got to know whether or not their President is a crook. Well, *I'm not a crook*." (Richard M. Nixon, November 11, 1973)

I'm sure you will understand
Help think up reasons you should believe me and trust me.

"I have not, and do not, intend to announce the timetable for our program, and there are obvious reasons for this decision which *I'm sure you will understand*. As I've indicated on several occasions, the rate of withdrawal [from Vietnam] will depend on developments." (Richard M. Nixon, November 3, 1969)

immigrants
Almost always to be praised and glorified, as long as from Europe.

"Tonight, as a son of *immigrants* with a wonderful wife and four terrific children, as a proud public servant who has cherished every minute of the last sixteen months on the campaign trail, I accept your nomination for the presidency of the United States." (Michael Dukakis, July 21, 1988)

"A son of *immigrants* and a grandson of *immigrants*— that's America, folks." (Michael Dukakis, July 22, 1988)

Antonym: *aliens*

imperialism
USAGE: Never American.

impotent
USAGE: Of course you are referring to powerlessness and not inability to have an erection—yet since the distinction will be blurry in the semiconscious minds of many, you should use this word at optimum times so the double entendre can only work to your advantage.

"In relation to Qadhafi, don't just make him mad. You have to render him *impotent*." (Pat Robertson, February 13, 1988)

Synonym: *wimp*

improprieties

Wrongdoing of belittled importance.

See also: *appearance of improprieties; indiscretion*

imprudent

USAGE: A splendid euphemism for describing blunders, bungled maneuvers, failed gambits, etc.

impunity, trampled with

USAGE: Remember that you can always say a bad-guy government has "trampled with impunity" after it invades another country; however, when the U.S. government finds certain invasions more congenial (e.g., Indonesia of East Timor and Israel of Lebanon) or conducts them (Grenada and Panama), it should go without saying that nothing of value is being trampled, with impunity or otherwise.

"First, fundamental principles of international law cannot be permitted to be *trampled with impunity*." (Senator Warren B. Rudman, January 12, 1991, just before voting to authorize the United States to attack Iraq.)

in charge

Synonym: *masterful*

Antonyms: *impotent; wimp*

in context

USAGE: If you're attacked for some past statements—or if you want to belittle the importance of objections to your policy position—say that they must be put "in context."

"That doesn't eliminate the real problems with nuclear energy. But they have to be viewed *in context*." (former senator Paul E. Tsongas, March 1991)

Antonym: out of context

inadvertent oversight
Antonym: *criminal neglect*

incentive for the enemy
USAGE: If you want to keep waging war, say that doing so provides "incentive for the enemy" to seek peace.

"An announcement of a fixed timetable for our withdrawal would completely remove any *incentive for the enemy* to negotiate an agreement. They would simply wait until our forces had withdrawn and then move in." (Richard M. Nixon, November 3, 1969)

incompetence
USAGE: Since incompetence seems to have become tacitly and widely accepted, denouncing it doesn't have as much sting these days.
     See also: *competence*

incomplete success
Failure.

incumbent
USAGE: A fairly neutral word for a current officeholder, but to be avoided if you are one. Don't remind them just how entrenched you are, or hope to be.

indiscretion
Downplayed malfeasance.
     See also: *improprieties*

individual, the value of the
A sacrosanct punch line for any number of political riddles.
USAGE: Whatever position you take on any issue, certainly

there will be ways to link it to your steadfast reverence for "the value of the individual."

"Ideologically, this 'Free Trade principle' destroys America's 200-year-old commitment to *the value of the individual* over all other values." (Representative Helen Delich Bentley, May 23, 1991)

individual initiative
USAGE: Always a good thing.
"The burden of tax revenues showed a similar pattern, with increasingly high tax rates stifling *individual initiative* and distorting the flow of saving and investment." (Ronald Reagan, February 10, 1982)
Antonyms: *paternalism; welfare*
See also: *productivity*

influence peddling
Antonym: *constituent services*
See also: *ethics*

In God We Trust
"The guiding principle and prayer of this nation has been, is now, and shall ever be, '*In God We Trust.*' " (John F. Kennedy, February 9, 1961)
See also: *E Pluribus Unum; God; under God*

innocent Americans
Imperiled citizens with a wholesome image, as distinct from imperiled citizens with a disparaged image.
USAGE: Can convey that you empathize with certain Americans, while some other Americans are less than innocent.
"Mr. President, for the sake of our children and grandchildren, we must begin treating AIDS as the public health concern it is. While some are using the AIDS issue to pro-

mote political and societal acceptance of an anti-Christian lifestyle, thousands of *innocent Americans* are dying." (Senator Jesse Helms, January 14, 1991)

See also: *anti-Christian; innocent victims of AIDS*

innocent children

Usually a subset of "innocent Americans."

USAGE: Sharpens the emotional insinuation that the "innocent" contrast with others less human.

"Is it not enough that the public health agenda of America has been torn apart by the AIDS movement, and that *innocent children*—like Ryan White—continue to die because the lobby and its allies promote civil rights rather than public safety?" (Senator Jesse Helms, January 14, 1991)

See also: *innocent victims of AIDS*

innocent victims of AIDS

Children, persons with hemophilia, transfusion recipients who contracted AIDS. A sleight-of-tongue way to blame other people with AIDS—gay men and IV drug users in particular—who are declared guilty by implication because they're not included in the "innocent" category.

insensitivity

USAGE: If you want to criticize a racist or sexist statement but don't want to risk being direct, simply decry the "insensitivity" involved. The word can likewise come in handy if you're under attack for uttering a racial or gender slur; you can express regret that some interpreted your comment as "insensitivity," thus perhaps smoothing ruffled feathers while not acknowledging there was much of a problem in the first place.

insiders

USAGE: If you're not in office, you can denounce "insiders." If you are, take pains to show that you aren't one.

See also: *Beltway, inside the*

instability

Commonly, any situation in the world that the U.S. government doesn't like.

See also: *stability*

insults

Incoming epithets, as distinct from outgoing epithets.

"The *insults* and distortions of Mr. Khrushchev—the violence of his attacks—shocked all Americans and united the country in admiration for the dignity of President Eisenhower." (John F. Kennedy, June 14, 1960)

integrity

USAGE: A standard description of qualities needed in a leader, which you fortunately just happen to have in abundance. The word can be used in various permutations with others that play to the images you've been laboring to cultivate.

"You've got to have an enormous amount of intellectual *integrity*—an understanding of who you are and where you want to lead the country and how you are going to get there." (Pierre S. du Pont IV, January 16, 1988)

"There can be no dissent from the principle that all officials must act with unwavering *integrity,* absolute impartiality and complete devotion to the public interest." (John F. Kennedy, April 27, 1961)

intellectuals, pointy-headed
USAGE: Reserve this expression for precincts where anti-academic sentiment runs high and few voters draw campus paychecks.

See also: *egghead*

intellectuals, vocal
Ivory-tower types who tend to be overly talkative.
USAGE: Can convey skepticism about academic thinkers without offending any.

"A small but growing group of *vocal intellectuals*—some conservative, some liberal—recommend that we legalize drugs and be done with the matter. . . . There are a great many reasons to oppose this argument." (Senator Dan Coats, September 1989)

intelligence
Data collection by the CIA and other espionage agencies. Not to be confused with smartness or wisdom.

"In the work of *intelligence,* heroes are undecorated and unsung, often even among their own fraternity. Their inspiration is rooted in patriotism. . . ." (Dwight D. Eisenhower, November 3, 1959, speaking at the cornerstone-laying for the CIA Building in Langley, Virginia.)

intelligence estimates
USAGE: When you want to buttress your policy position but don't have facts to back it up, you can cite "intelligence estimates." Since people expect such estimates to be secretive, it's unlikely you'll be pressed for details.

intelligence gathering
Spying.

internal affairs
A term as slippery as the beaches of the Bay of Pigs, the Dominican Republic, Grenada, and Panama.

"I realize that it will always be a cardinal tenet of American foreign policy not to intervene in the *internal affairs* of other nations—and that this is particularly true in Latin America." (John F. Kennedy, December 15, 1958)

international law
USAGE: Don't hesitate to extol "international law," but you'll probably want to ignore specific verdicts from world bodies condemning actions by the U.S. government and its closest allies—such as certain judgments rendered by the International Court of Justice in The Hague and certain resolutions passed by the U.N. General Assembly. Take care not to acknowledge that the United States has refused to accept those decisions.

"Our commitment to *international law* and to international organizations has been demonstrated anew." (Senator Richard G. Lugar, January 17, 1991)

"*International law* provides the basis for action when one country invades another." (Senator Bill Bradley, April 15, 1991)

"The Israeli possession of Judaea and Samaria has stronger claim to validity under *international law* and historical precedent than that of any Arab state. As a Baptist, I feel very strongly about that." (Senator Jesse Helms, July 26, 1991)

See also: *outlaw nation; rule of law*

intolerance

USAGE: When you find a certain viewpoint intolerable, you might consider accusing its most outspoken adherents of "intolerance."

"We all should be alarmed at the rise of *intolerance* in our land, and by the growing tendency to use intimidation rather than reason in settling disputes." (George Bush, May 4, 1991)

See also: *political correctness*

intolerance of Christianity

USAGE: A verbal form of Bible-thumping, such language plays well for many fundamentalist constituents.

"Instead of engendering an official attitude of neutrality toward religion in the schools as the public was led to believe they would, those [U.S. Supreme Court] decisions have in fact fueled the flames of Government *intolerance of Christianity* in the public schools." (Senator Jesse Helms, January 14, 1991)

Caution: Distinctly inadvisable for areas with substantial Jewish populations.

See also: *anti-Christian; barring God from our classrooms*

intransigent

Overly independent and inhospitable to manipulation.

"Taking an attitude of neither servile submission nor *intransigent* nationalism, you have cooperated with the mainland and the Federal Government to the mutual benefit of us all." (John F. Kennedy, December 15, 1958, speaking in Puerto Rico.)

involuntary immigrants

Slaves.

USAGE: Smooths over a momentous jagged edge of American history.

"Most immigrants came to America precisely in order to escape their pasts. They wanted to participate in the making of an American culture and an American national identity. Even black Americans, who came as *involuntary immigrants* and have suffered—still suffer—awful persecution and discrimination, have made vital contributions to the American culture." (Historian and former presidential speechwriter Arthur Schlesinger, Jr., June 25, 1991)

Iron Curtain

Obsolete.

irresponsible

A generic adjective of condemnation.

USAGE: Once you get used to it, you'll be amazed at how many people and organizations you can call "irresponsible."

Is there an echo in here?

USAGE: When heckling becomes too obvious to ignore.

"We must continue to improve our defenses if we're to preserve peace and freedom. This is—*Is there an echo in here?*" (Ronald Reagan, June 9, 1982, in response to protesters shouting about El Salvador and other subjects in the midst of his speech to the Bundestag in Bonn.)

I've never been accused of being a genius

I don't have an ego problem, or put on airs.

USAGE: A humility statement par excellence. Appropriately

self-effacing. In some contexts, might appeal to voters who resent people they perceive as intellectuals.

"I'm not a brilliant person. I do produce some good legislation. But *I've never been accused of being a genius.* But I feel that being there and making the vote is my duty and responsibility." (Representative Charles E. Bennett, June 6, 1991)

jobs jobs jobs
Carrots carrots carrots to dangle dangle dangle.

"This will be the absolute center of high energy physics for the entire world. The only thing comparable in the past in Texas has been our space center. This just means we have taken a great step forward in our scientific endeavors. It's good, good for Texas *jobs, jobs, jobs.*" (Texas governor Bill Clements, November 10, 1988)

Joe Six-packs
Apt to be solicitous and contemptuous, this term refers to stereotypic working class, marginally schooled white males, who presumably drink tap rather than mineral water and standard American beer rather than suave imports. One of the galleries that electoral strategists routinely play to; highly regarded for numerical strength in many precincts. Various sorts of simplemindedness can be projected onto this group, serving a convenient pretense that narrow patterns of thought are less prevalent among the upper classes. USAGE: The expression evokes a fraying white T-shirt, beer can in hand, empties strewn across the living room floor in front of the television, and monosyllables shouted into the kitchen. Depending on the context, audience, and intonation, "Joe Six-packs" can be heard as a respectful reference to populist sentiment, or might be interpreted as down-the-nose mockery of average working people. You may want to

confine use of this term to private flippancy or savvy not-for-attribution remarks to journalists.

"If Dukakis pulls a Mondale, there are a lot of *Joe Six-packs* around the country who are going to say, 'Uh-oh, look who's kissing Jesse's rear end.' " (A "top Democratic campaign operative, who asked not to be identified," quoted in *The Washington Post,* July 16, 1988)

"These people do not fit the stereotype of who identifies with us. These guys are *Joe Six-packs.*" (Jesse Jackson, August 15, 1991)

Judeo-Christian
USAGE: A tidy catchphrase for conveying that one is of a biblical frame of mind, and savvy enough not to turn off Jewish voters.

"I was trying to suggest that we also, in a *Judeo-Christian* society and in a democracy, we need values to be taught to our children." (Representative Jack Kemp, December 19, 1987)

jump to conclusions
What certain other politicians and some critics are prone to do.

just and lasting peace
The kind that warmakers perennially claim to be seeking.

"I have initiated a plan which will end this war in a way that will bring us closer to that great goal to which Woodrow Wilson and every American President in our history has been dedicated—the goal of a *just and lasting peace.*" (Richard M. Nixon, November 3, 1969)

"There is no one more devoted, more committed to the hard work of freedom, than every soldier and sailor, every Marine, airman, and Coastguardsman—every man and woman now serving in the Persian Gulf. Each of them has volunteered to provide for this nation's defense—and now they bravely struggle, to earn for America, for the world, and for the future generations, a *just and lasting peace.*" (George Bush, January 29, 1991)

See also: *lasting peace*

just punishment
See: *law and order*

just say no
Just be simplistic about drug use.

Derivation: Popularized by Nancy Reagan during her hubby's presidency.

See also: *drug-free America*

just war
USAGE: Any war you like. (Of course, you'll need to come up with a better definition in public.)

"In order for a war to be just . . . there must be an advancement of good and avoidance of evil. Judging by these criteria, Operation Desert Storm truly is a *just war.*" (Dan Quayle, February 7, 1991)

Kk Ll

"K" is for Kinder Gentler
"L" is for Lean

keep the peace
Advice with any number of underlying agendas.

"*Keep the peace,* and then we will do what is right for you." (Secretary of the Interior Jacob D. Cox, June 1870, addressing Sioux chief Red Cloud and other Indian leaders at a meeting in Washington, D.C.)

"Look at the candidates on the basis of what is best for America and what leader can best *keep the peace.*" (Richard M. Nixon, March 1960)

Kennedy, being compared to John F.
USAGE: Such comparisons are to be encouraged, and are not hard to come by. Obviously being a Democrat who hails from Massachusetts is a plus, but not necessary. Almost any male politician under sixty with decent speechwriters and a healthy head of hair should consider this accolade to be within reach, if he can speak assertively while affecting some kind of brainy wit and vigor. If you can convince people that you read voraciously from the classics to modern history, gaining a reputation as a sparkling intellect shouldn't be too tough. (Just ask George Will.) Pulling sagacious aphorisms from Bartlett's *Familiar Quotations* may suffice.

"Mike is *being compared to John F. Kennedy.* He is from Massachusetts. He has chosen a running mate from Texas, and he's going to defeat an incumbent Republican Vice President." (Jimmy Carter, July 18, 1988)

Antonym: *Kennedy, you're no Jack*

Kennedy, you're no Jack
Even Jack Kennedy was no Jack Kennedy.

Derivation: Lloyd Bentsen's riposte in the 1988 vice presidential debate, when he told Dan Quayle, "You're no Jack Kennedy."

Antonym: *Kennedy, being compared to John F.*

kick ass
USAGE: Keep private. And watch out for mikes.

"We tried to *kick* a little *ass* last night . . . Whoops, oh God, he heard me. Turn that thing off." (George Bush, speaking on the morning after his vice presidential debate with Geraldine Ferraro in October 1984, at first unaware that a TV-boom microphone was picking up his words.)

"If you ever keep Hubert waiting again, I'll *kick* your *ass* down that hall." (Lyndon B. Johnson, quoted in the August 1967 issue of *Esquire* magazine)

See also: *balls; stick*

kinder gentler
Contrary to some previous perceptions, not callous.

USAGE: A good way to proclaim compassionate desires along the way to explaining that you're not about to support a lot of government spending to help people. You can beat this rhetorical bongo endlessly.

"I want a *kinder, gentler* nation." (George Bush, August 18, 1988)

"When I talked of a *kinder, gentler* nation, I wasn't trying to just create a slogan. I was issuing a challenge. An effective government must know its limitations and respect its people's capabilities. In return, people must assume the final burden of freedom—and that's responsibility." (George Bush, May 4, 1991)

See also: *responsibility*

knee-jerk
Reactions not approved of.

kooks
Disfavored people with strongly expressed views.

"*kooks* . . . demagogues . . . social misfits . . ." (Spiro Agnew, referring to defendants in the Chicago Eight trial, 1970)

Antonym: *patriots*

See also: *fanatics; zealots*

labels
Concise and mostly negative tags pinned on politicians, usually by their foes.

USAGE: Claim to eschew labels, since you prefer to engage in straight talk and substantive discussion of the real issues. If labeled in an injurious way, you may want to respond that you're not into labels; this does not in any way foreclose your options for plastering opponents with pejorative labels at other times. If all else fails, try labeling your opponent a compulsive labeler.

"Political *labels* will not influence thinking citizens." (Dwight D. Eisenhower, September 16, 1961)

"I don't believe in characterizing people with *labels*. I think you do a great disservice when you engage in name-calling. . . . And I would not want to *label* people who agree with me or disagree with me." (Lyndon B. Johnson, April 27, 1965)

". . . this election is . . . not about meaningless *labels.*" (Michael Dukakis, July 21, 1988)

"If the Vice President wants to spend all his time talking about *labels,* he can do so." (Michael Dukakis, July 22, 1988)

See also: *ideologues; orthodoxies, stale*

labor bosses, big
Politicians using this label rarely refer to "big business bosses."

USAGE: Union leaders whom you don't like and/or who have endorsed your opponent.

"This ad is just one aspect of an emotionally charged and misleading campaign to garner support for a bill that *big labor bosses* are dying to see become law." (Representative Andy Ireland, July 17, 1991)

labor rights
USAGE: Naturally, sometimes you will want to speak out for them in certain societies. But you'll probably want to be more "evenhanded" when it comes to conflicts between owners and workers in the Third World—and, of course, in the United States.

See also: *evenhanded*

laid a glove on
Caught.

"They haven't *laid a glove on* him [CIA director William Casey]. . . . I have yet to hear or see any credible evidence that would lead me to believe Mr. Casey should resign." (Senator Lloyd M. Bentsen, July 1981)

land reform

USAGE: A good idea, abstractly speaking, for some countries. Not applicable to the United States.

lasting peace

Upcoming hypothetical peace of a duration supposedly commensurate with, and worth, all the suffering and costs sure to result from current military escalation.

"Let them [white hunters] kill, skin, and sell until the buffalo is exterminated, as it is the only way to bring *lasting peace* and allow civilization to advance." (General Philip Sheridan, early 1870s) According to historian Dee Brown, "Of the 3,700,000 buffalo destroyed from 1872 through 1874, only 150,000 were killed by Indians."

"On the foundation of our victory we can build a *lasting peace.* . . ." (Harry S Truman, January 21, 1946)

"As surely as we seek *lasting peace,* we shall find it only as . . ." (Dwight D. Eisenhower, August 6, 1953)

"Because of America's bold initiatives, 1972 will be long remembered as the year of the greatest progress since the end of World War II toward a *lasting peace* in the world." (Richard M. Nixon, January 20, 1973)

"I would hope that the nations of the world might say that we had built a *lasting peace,* built not on weapons of war but on international policies which reflect our own most precious values." (Jimmy Carter, January 20, 1977)

"We have and will continue to struggle for a *lasting peace* that enhances dignity for men and women everywhere." (Ronald Reagan, January 16, 1984)

"Authorizing the use of force . . . is a step in the direction of *lasting peace.* . . ." (Representative William S. Broomfield, January 12, 1991)

"We've got to put this victory and the influence and power it will bring to some great and noble purpose. And I believe that purpose is trying to get a *lasting peace* in the Middle East." (Senator Phil Gramm, February 11, 1991)

See also: *diplomacy; just and lasting peace*

law and order

Usually a quantitative measure. Applied to stopping crime in the streets but not in the suites.

USAGE: Your concern here is to have voters identify you as belonging to a tradition that ranges from Wyatt Earp to the proverbial cop on the beat.

"I believe that the overwhelming majority of Americans will join in preserving *law and order* and reject resolutely those who espouse violence no matter what the cause." (Lyndon B. Johnson, July 21, 1964, commenting on riots in New York City.)

"In a democracy such as ours, the preservation of *law and order* begins with the individual." (Hubert H. Humphrey, May 25, 1966, speaking at graduation exercises of the FBI National Academy.)

"Who is responsible for the breakdown of *law and order* in this country?" (Richard M. Nixon, August 15, 1966)

"What we have to do in America is generate a great belief in democracy. One of the things it demands is respect for *law and order*." (Dwight D. Eisenhower, November 1966)

See also: *violence*

leader of the world

USAGE: When it isn't enough to describe the president as the leader of the most powerful nation in the world.

"He [White House chief of staff John Sununu] is the key operating officer for the *leader of the world*." (Representative Newt Gingrich, June 25, 1991)

leadership

A timeworn buzzword that politicians use to pat themselves on the back, offering definitions they just happen to be claiming to fulfill.

"What America needs is new *leadership*." (Richard M. Nixon, November 6, 1966)

"*Leadership* today requires the ability to lead and inspire others—to lead and inspire in a sense of common enterprise." (Hubert H. Humphrey, January 6, 1967)

leak

Selective and anonymous conduiting of information to news media. Not to be confused with urination.

USAGE: No matter how much you leak to the press, you should publicly assume a posture of having never leaked anything. Such an activity would be beneath you (though not, evidently, beneath your opponents).

lean

Adjective often used in tandem with a euphemism for deadly.

"It's time to clean up those Pentagon scandals and build a *lean,* tough, competent military force." (Jimmy Carter, July 18, 1988)

See also: *lean and mean*

lean and mean

High praise for the U.S. military. Efficient killing power.

left field

A mixed sports/politics metaphor. Although a legitimate position in either realm, this is a light-touch jab in the pugilistic style of Joe McCarthy.

"I just think them [the American Civil Liberties Union]

to be way out in deep *left field.*" (George Bush, July 22, 1988)

left-wing
To some minds a pejorative.
  Antonym: *right-wing*

legitimate government
A foreign government legitimized by the U.S. government's approval.
  "I have proposed to the Congress that no new canal administrator be appointed unless and until the President of the United States certifies to Congress that the Panamanian government is elected according to the procedures of its own constitution. In other words, the canal administrator must be selected by a *legitimate government,* and not Noriega's drug dictatorship." (Senator Dan Coats, May 1989)

less fortunate
A genteel term for people who've been shafted by social inequities.
  "Jackson's campaign has been one of striving for the *less fortunate. . . .*" (Democratic National Committee chair Paul G. Kirk, Jr., July 18, 1988)
  "New initiatives in child care, education and welfare are all designed to give *less fortunate* Americans a stake in their future." (Representative Harris W. Fawell, July 15, 1991)
  See also: *disadvantaged; underprivileged*

let us
The first two words of innumerable political invocations that amount to pronouncements and would-be directives put forward with an aura of request and benediction.

"All this will not be finished in the first 100 days. Nor will it be finished in the first 1,000 days, nor in the life of this Administration, nor even perhaps in our lifetime on this planet. But *let us* begin." (John F. Kennedy, January 20, 1961)

"*Let us* now join reason to faith and action to experience, to transform our unity of interest into a unity of purpose." (Lyndon B. Johnson, January 20, 1965)

"*Let us* be proud that our system has produced and provided more freedom and more abundance, more widely shared, than any other system in the history of the world. *Let us* be proud that in each of the four wars in which we have been engaged in this century, including the one we are now bringing to an end, we have fought not for our selfish advantage, but to help others resist aggression. *Let us* be proud that . . ." (Richard M. Nixon, January 20, 1973)

let us reason together
At least until I decide that I need to use force to get my way.
USAGE: With suitable intonation, can make a speechmaker sound a bit like a prophet.

"The people of the world, I think, prefer reasoned agreement to ready attack. That is why we must follow the Prophet Isaiah many, many times before we send the Marines, and say, 'Come now, *let us reason together.*'" (Lyndon B. Johnson, March 24, 1964)

Derivation: Old Testament

level playing field
A generic appeal for fairness—or for a less-than-fair angle termed "level."

"I believe that if the United States can trade with other nations on a *level playing field,* we can out-produce, out-

compete, and out-sell anybody, anywhere in the world."
(Ronald Reagan, February 6, 1986)

"You and I know that if the *playing field* is *level,* America's workers and farmers can out-work and out-produce anyone, anytime, anywhere." (George Bush, January 29, 1991)

"Will [a free-trade pact with Mexico] *level* the *playing field* or leave it tilted in such a way that there will be a net loss of American jobs?" (Senator Carl M. Levin, 1991)

"We must *level* the *playing field.* . . . We must give our companies a more *level playing field* through policy changes that don't require massive federal expenditures." (former senator Paul E. Tsongas, March 1991)

Antonym: *uneven playing field*
See also: *fair play*

liberal
Antonym (sort of): *conservative*

liberal, bleeding-heart
See: *bleeding heart*

liberal media
A mythological concept of the Fourth Estate as a bastion of muckraking fervor.
USAGE: Assuming you're among the vast majority of politicians who have no intention of upsetting corporate apple carts, you might want to blame the "liberal media" if you are troubled by even mildly critical press coverage. That's a good move for distracting from the content of criticisms. And most news media, being stolidly tied to the status quo, will keep falling all over themselves to show that they're not "liberal."

liberation
USAGE: Reference to the overthrow or displacement of any government you don't like.

liberty
Often depicted as inert and total in the United States, as if "liberty" were some kind of national possession. Constant use of the term obscures social conditions that are distinctly lacking in liberty.

"A continental nation blessed with *liberty,* natural resources and a diverse people . . ." (Senator Bill Bradley, 1990)

"Our party system remains as one of the massive foundations of our *liberty.*" (Harry S Truman, March 23, 1946)

lie
USAGE: Do not acknowledge under any circumstances that you've ever told a "lie." Always be adamant, if pressed, that "lie" is something you would never dream of doing. Practice euphemisms such as "I misspoke" for worst-case scenarios. Be creative!

"There are times, obviously, when the President can't tell the public everything that he's asked. And on many occasions, if the news people just happened to ask a question about something that I thought ought to be kept secret for a while, I would say, 'Well, I can't answer that.' But during the four years I was in office, I never told the people a *lie.*" (Jimmy Carter, November 28, 1987)

See also: *bodyguard of lies; misspoke*

lifted us up
A narrative metaphor for a favorable experience of leadership.
USAGE: Summons to many minds the fond memories of be-

ing lifted from the ground by parents, grandparents, and other older relatives who seemed to offer beneficent protection.

"I feel very comfortable with President Reagan's priorities. I think he's *lifted us up* and given this country a respect around the world." (George Bush, December 5, 1987)

limiting government

Cutting social programs (but not military programs).

"Republicans know that America is great because of what a free people had the chance to do for themselves, and by *limiting government,* we can provide unlimited opportunities to people, the engine of prosperity, and the source of liberty." (Representative Guy Vander Jagt, February 22, 1990)

See also: *big government; enhancing the role of the individual; voluntarism*

line-item veto

High on the charts of the economic panacea hit parade: presidential power to pick and choose among specific spending items within a single appropriations bill.

USAGE: Since implementing such a setup would confer enormous new power on the president, avoid any reference to that aspect of the proposed change if you're pushing it.

"And what we need is a constitutional amendment that requires a balanced budget. And we want one that goes with it—that I had as governor, 43 governors of our 50 states have—it's called a *line-item veto.*" (Ronald Reagan, November 28, 1987)

"The *line-item veto* will give the President the knife to cut out this fat." (Representative William S. Broomfield, January 3, 1991)

linkage

The wrong connections; insufficient fragmentation of awareness; failure to accept favored hypocrisy.

"The Palestinian issue is serious and must be resolved. But no rational thinker believes there is a *linkage*. The invasion of Kuwait was a separate act of Iraqi aggression. . . ." (Representative Steve Schiff, January 11, 1991)

little minds

Belittled minds of foes.

"Men of *little minds* are trying to make this a political issue." (Senator Joseph R. McCarthy, October 1, 1951)

lobbyists

USAGE: If you refer to "lobbyists" in public, you should do so with some evident distaste. The lobbyists who arrange matters such as contributions to your campaigns will understand that some postured distance is in order and mutually advantageous. What they want is your cooperation, not public embraces.

"In fact a number of legislators, unions and other *lobbyists* have already made income tax increases their principal thrust. I am opposed to these tax increases." (New York governor Mario M. Cuomo, February 13, 1991)

"It is time for us to take a new look at our own government, to strip away the secrecy, to expose the unwarranted pressure of *lobbyists*, to eliminate waste. . . ." (Jimmy Carter, July 15, 1976)

"An uninformed president, fronting for the big-time *lobbyists*, shouldn't be in the White House. That's what they [Republicans] are trying to sell you this year. Don't you buy it." (Harry S Truman, October 5, 1952)

long knives
The wrong knives, pointed in the wrong direction.

"That's four Senate confirmations. But sadly, that doesn't matter to those lining up against him. And they've got their *long knives* ready." (Dan Quayle, July 17, 1991, speaking of U.S. Supreme Court nominee Clarence Thomas.)

long-term strength
Usually a reference to military dominance.

"This effort was doomed to failure because we have failed for the past eight years to build the positions of *long-term strength* essential to successful negotiation." (John F. Kennedy, June 14, 1960)

loony left
A British import, popular with Tories in England, that conservatives can use to label strong opponents as beyond reason.

lose the peace
Fail to dominate the peacetime situation.

"The general consensus is that we shouldn't *lose the peace* by walking away from a significant foreign-policy success." (Unnamed "Administration official" quoted by Associated Press, June 11, 1991, commenting on plans to continue sending covert U.S. aid to Angolan guerrillas in 1992 despite a new pact to end Angola's sixteen-year civil war.)

Antonym: *win the peace*

love
A many-splendored rhetorical thing.

"I *love* this land and cherish its future. I want to set about making this country a great, decent, and good land. . . ." (George McGovern, June 14, 1972)

"The poor, the aged, the weak, the afflicted must be treated with respect and compassion and with *love.* I have spoken a lot of times this year about *love.* But *love* must be aggressively translated into simple justice." (Jimmy Carter, July 15, 1976)

"There is, as [Senator] Pete [Domenici] so eloquently said, in the American heart a spirit of *love,* of caring, and a willingness to work together." (Ronald Reagan, February 4, 1982)

low income
Poor.

low-intensity conflict
"Low intensity" except for the people being bombed, strafed, kidnapped, tortured, etc.

loyal
Dependably obedient. A prized political attribute. Questions are rarely asked, such as: To what? For what purposes? At what costs?

"He [Bobby Baker] is a man who truly serves his country, and I consider him one of my most trusted, most *loyal,* and most competent friends." (Lyndon B. Johnson, August 30, 1957)

loyal opposition
Cooperation with the party in power by the party with less power—a stance that usually involves much more loyalty than opposition.
USAGE: A handy phrase to rationalize habitually kowtowing to powers-that-be.

"I've always had this attitude that a party ought to be the *loyal opposition*. Winning is an important goal, but winning isn't the only goal." (Iowa attorney general and former Iowa Democratic Party chair Bonnie Campbell, April 1991)

"To my friends—and yes, I do mean friends—in the *loyal opposition*—and yes, I mean loyal: I put out my hand. I am putting out my hand to you, Mr. Speaker. I am putting out my hand to you, Mr. Majority Leader." (George Bush, January 20, 1989)

lust
Warning: Keep it to yourself. As Jimmy Carter demonstrated in an interview published by *Playboy* magazine in autumn 1976, such a topic can cause big trouble if candidly discussed on the record. ("I've looked on a lot of women with lust. I've committed adultery in my heart many times.")

lynch mob atmosphere
Discomfiting critical attention.

"I do not favor violations of ethics or laws at all in or out of government, but I do want to call your attention to one thing. I think—and this has gone on pretty much throughout the time that I've been here—that there is a kind of *lynch mob atmosphere* that takes place, and people are—the memories are there of this person, that person, and so forth." (Ronald Reagan, February 24, 1988)

Mm Nn

"M" is for More Will Than Wallet
"N" is for Naked Aggression

madman

A foreign leader who is to be totally objectified, as if lacking any rationality.

USAGE: Particularly helpful for describing someone whose country is high on the list of potential targets for U.S. military attack.

"My sentiment was that we should have taken him [Qadhafi] prisoner, gone after him, somehow taken his power base away from him. Or killed him. I wouldn't have hesitated to kill him. He's a *madman* and he was a terrorist and he declared war on the United States." (Pat Robertson, February 13, 1988)

Caution: Guard against overuse, since verbal inflation can reduce the impact of this label. And it can be especially embarrassing to build an alliance later with someone dubbed a "madman," since a foreign leader could less plausibly be said to have recovered from insanity than, say, from ideological extremism or a contempt for human rights.

See also: *declared war on the United States*

magic of America

A would-be national spirit of secular religiosity.

USAGE: Can evoke the chief executive as a kind of President Houdini.

"We must carry forward the *magic of America.*" (George Bush, June 12, 1991)

See also: *dreams can come true for all of us*

majesty

USAGE: Can evoke regal grandeur and sovereigns, even while seeming simply enthusiastic for God and country.

"The President . . . represents the *majesty* of the law and of the people as fully and as essentially, and with the same dignity, as does any absolute monarch or the head of any independent government in the world." (Attorney General Henry Stanbery, 1867)

"I ask you to share with me today the *majesty* of this moment." (Richard M. Nixon, January 20, 1969)

"I see an America on the move again . . . an America that lives up to the *majesty* of our Constitution and the simple decency of our people." (Jimmy Carter, July 15, 1976)

See also: *cathedral of the spirit*

manifest destiny

USAGE: A term of declining popularity due to its notoriety as a code for methodical massacres of native peoples, but still offering rhetorical convenience on occasion.

The U.S.A. is a country of "*manifest destiny.*" (Richard M. Nixon, November 3, 1969)

See: *American century, the next; American way, the*

manipulating

USAGE: Must be described as profoundly abhorrent.

"The thought of somebody *manipulating* people for his own good, that just disgusts me to even consider it." (Pat Robertson, February 13, 1988)

market economy
Has come to mean socialism for the rich: privatized profits and socialized risks.

USAGE: Equate a "market economy" with freedom, and skim over fine points such as inequities, exploitative relationships between owners and workers, unemployment, poverty, etc. Don't stumble into mentioning that the loudest enthusiasts for a "market economy" are the ones in a position to profit most from one. If such objections are raised, label the skeptic an "ideologue."

". . . we are a nation based on a *market economy* and a belief in individual freedom. . . . Government has a role to stimulate the private-sector economy. But in the United States of America for 200 years, the *market economy* has been the engine of our opportunity, and it has been the insignia for freedom for the American people." (Pierre S. du Pont IV, January 16, 1988)

". . . and I can tell you I just returned from the Soviet Union and from Europe and many people there are proud of the movement of democracy and *market economics* that is sweeping the world." (Arkansas governor Bill Clinton, June 15, 1991)

Antonym: *command economy*

See also: *free markets; free markets and free peoples; ideologues; opportunity*

market reform
A plethora of economic changes that would open a country's economy to investment—and leverage—from afar, whether by companies such as ITT, IBM, and GE, or agencies such as the International Monetary Fund and the World Bank.

"I hope President Gorbachev now brings forward a new effort at serious *market reform*. The door to the Euro-Atlantic community is open. But only the Soviets can decide to step over the threshold." (Secretary of State James A. Baker III, June 18, 1991)

marketplace
Makes the multinational corporate arena sound as folksy, accessible, and open to newcomers as a neighborhood farmers' market.

"We are daily witnessing this ever-mounting national debt, the inexorable sale of America to foreign interests, and the steady deterioration of our capacity to compete in the global *marketplace*." (former senator Paul E. Tsongas, March 1991)

marketplace of ideas
A pat concept of intellectual commerce, encouraging persistent notions that people should be shopping for ethical, moral, analytical, and political products in much the same way that they might purchase items such as hair spray, toothpaste, or automobiles.

"So if our young people—or anyone else for that matter —wish to criticize, I defend that. But they must also be willing to listen while others speak; and they must be willing to have their views tested in the *marketplace of ideas*." (Robert F. Kennedy, November 5, 1965)

massive invasion into the confidentiality of
Could expose what I did.

"Thus, it is clear that the continued succession of demands for additional Presidential conversations has become a never-ending process, and that to continue providing these conversations in response to the constantly escalating requests would constitute such a *massive invasion into the confidentiality of* Presidential conversations that the institutions of the Presidency itself would be fatally compromised." (Richard M. Nixon, May 22, 1974)

See also: *fatally weaken this office*

masterful
Proven worthy of being our master.

"Moreover, the President's personal relationships with the leaders of the allied states are unparalleled. Having *masterfully* forged a fragile multinational coalition, he is the one who can best gauge its cohesion and durability." (Senator Warren B. Rudman, January 12, 1991)

Synonym: *in charge*

may well be
A hedgephrase suitable for preceding brazen inventions.

"[The Soviets] *may well be* pulling ahead of us in numbers of long-range jet bombers with a nuclear bomb capacity." (John F. Kennedy, November 13, 1959)

maybe they'll change
Shrug.

"I'm not going to protest Burning Tree. *Maybe they'll change.* I think it would be a good idea for them to take women into the club. I don't have any problem playing there in the meantime." (Dan Quayle, December 1990)

McCarthyism
Formerly the scurrilous use of smear tactics to impute disloyalty and Communist subversion. Now the accusation of "McCarthyism" is so scattered that it can be used as a blunderbuss by just about anyone who wants to snipe at political adversaries.

McCarthyism, the new
See: *political correctness*

meaningful, make an election
USAGE: Of course you're concerned about what's "meaningful" to you—but if you want to pass judgment on the meaning of an election, there's no need to be candid about your underlying criteria. After all, a big factor as to whether you consider an election to be "meaningful" is your attitude toward the government administering it; however, you can hardly spell that out in public.

"The important thing is that if there is to be an electoral process, it be observed not only at the moment when people vote, but in all the preliminary aspects that *make an election meaningful.*" (Secretary of State George P. Shultz, February 5, 1984, speaking about Nicaraguan elections. Shultz did not apply similar precepts that same year, or later, to U.S.-backed elections in neighboring Guatemala and El Salvador, where human rights abuses were rampant.)

meat-ax approach
Antonyms: cut out fat; *streamline*

melting pot
An oratorical recipe for America, without mentioning that those at the bottom are most likely to get burned.

"In the *melting pot* of America we have not tried to shape everything according to one pattern. Rather, we have welcomed all and have all shared in the diversity and richness that each has to contribute." (Richard M. Nixon, October 18, 1956)

"Only in the case of the Negro has the *melting pot* failed

to bring a minority into the full stream of American life."
(John F. Kennedy, 1959)

men
The male gender projected as all humanity. Still a common
password for the political clubhouse.

The Declaration of Independence "gave promise that in
due time the weights would be lifted from the shoulders of
all *men,* and that all should have an equal chance." (Abraham Lincoln)

"The final battle against intolerance is to be fought—not
in the chambers of any legislature—but in the hearts of
men." (Dwight D. Eisenhower, October 19, 1956)

"And when at some future date the high court of history
sits in judgment on each of us, recording whether in our
brief span of service we fulfilled our responsibilities to the
state, our success or failure, in whatever office we hold, will
be measured by the answers to four questions: First, were
we truly *men* of courage . . . Second, were we truly *men* of
judgment . . . Third, were we truly *men* of integrity . . .
Finally, were we truly *men* of dedication?" (John F. Kennedy, January 9, 1961)

"If today there is a proper American 'sphere of influence' it is this fragile sphere called earth upon which all
men live and share a common fate—a sphere where our
influence must be for peace and justice." (Hubert H. Humphrey, January 6, 1967)

"For freedom has an inevitability of its own—an inevitability rooted, not in the myth of a communist dialectic, but
in the highest hopes of common *men.*" (Senator Dan Coats,
June 1989)

middle class
A category—often intentionally vague—blurring distinctions between households with annual incomes of $20,000 or $100,000.

"Opportunity for all also means that the government ought to help the *middle class* as well as the poor when they need it." (Arkansas governor Bill Clinton, May 6, 1991)

"In effect the *middle class* and the working poor have been called upon to pay for the huge income tax cuts at the federal level." (New York governor Mario M. Cuomo, August 9, 1991)

militant
Overly active for a particular cause being frowned upon.

"The existing immigration law works for the good of all the American people; it must not be treated like a special interest football to be kicked around at the whim of any *militant* group and its apologists in government." (Senator Jesse Helms, January 14, 1991)

Synonym: *radical*

Antonyms: *moderate; responsible*

militarism
Militarism of certain other countries.

USAGE: For practical political purposes, the United States is incapable of this evil. Bite your tongue.

"We cannot tolerate this approach, Mr. President. Not only would it extend an award to the Iraqis for their *militarism,* but it would also . . ." (Senator John Seymour, January 12, 1991)

"The best thing Iraq can do now is get rid of its current political leadership. They must choose between continuing down its fruitless path of *militarism* led by Hussein or turn

inward and construct a new nation dedicated to peace."
(Representative Duncan Hunter, February 28, 1991)

military dictator
Out of favor with the U.S. government.
  Antonym: *military leader*

military leader
A military dictator in favor with the U.S. government.
  Antonyms: *military dictator;* military strongman

military preparedness
Often, military aggressiveness.
  "War is the most difficult test of a nation. It tests a nation's *military preparedness.* It tests the productivity of its economy. It tests . . ." (Richard M. Nixon, June 1966)
  Synonym: *armed vigilance*
  See also: *deterrence; resolve*

military reform
See: *lean and mean; reforms*

mine field
Can figure into an ultimate comeback against journalists and others who give voice to annoying skepticism about U.S. military actions.
  "Ever been in a *mine field*? All there's gotta be is one mine, and that's intense." (General Norman Schwarzkopf, late February 1991, responding to a question at a press briefing in Saudi Arabia.)

minor violation
See: *improprieties; indiscretion*

missile gap
One of history's bogus "gaps" used by the ambitious (in this case, JFK) to con the gullible (guess who?).

"And most important of all—and most tragically ironic— our nation could have afforded, and can afford now, the steps necessary to close the *missile gap*." (John F. Kennedy, August 14, 1958)

misspoke
USAGE: Nobody's perfect. Sooner or later you're going to get your lines tangled or your stories mixed up. Some pushy reporter at a press conference, or loudmouth constituent at a town meeting, will start to nail you. Don't panic. Try the usual stratagems. If you find yourself getting in deeper, here's a verbal lifeline: "I misspoke." It's not elegant, but it should suffice for extrication purposes.
See also: *clarify*

misunderstandings
Conflicts that now can be subordinated to mutually advantageous agendas.
USAGE: When long-running clashes seem to have outlived their usefulness, stress the need to overcome past "misunderstandings" in order to achieve a cooperative working relationship. You always have the option of going back to a more combative stance later on.

"Our challenge is to communicate across *misunderstandings* to unify our party and to challenge our nation." (Jesse Jackson, July 15, 1988)
Synonym: miscommunication
See also: *friends; misspoke*

moderate

Not disrupting favored scenarios. Often a reasonable facade masking a status quo that is corrupt or oppressive.

"The hardest job for a politician today is to have the courage to be *moderate*." (Hubert H. Humphrey, 1965)

"We would see an assault on the *moderate* Arab states and on Israel. . . . Who will suffer if the United States fails to step up to this issue? Certainly the *moderate* Arab states would." (Senator Orrin G. Hatch, January 12, 1991)

"Thus, we must strengthen the hand of South African whites, Asians, Coloreds, and *moderate* blacks in the forthcoming negotiations for a new constitution. . . . To do any less, is to join those who really wanted revolution and a resultant one-party state in that country." (Senator Jesse Helms, February 26, 1991)

Synonym: *responsible*
Antonyms: *militant; radical*
See also: *our allies*

modern weapons systems

The latest in highly profitable weaponry, usually nuclear, with missiles that are faster, more accurate, and more likely to reduce response times for the other side's commanders —permitting them only a few minutes to determine whether they're actually under attack before deciding about a launch of their own missiles.

USAGE: "Modern" has a pleasant ring to it, connoting user-friendly, convenient, state-of-the-art, perhaps smartly stylish. Thus a reassuring modifier for new thermonuclear weapons.

"Jimmy Carter . . . supported *modern weapons systems* —the cruise missile, the Stealth bomber and the Trident submarine—and he did it without waste and without scandal." (former secretary of state Edmund S. Muskie, July 18, 1988)

See also: *modernization; nuclear stockpile, total*

modernization

USAGE: Say "modernization" or "modernize" when referring to new American deployments of nuclear arms and other weaponry. Do not use this benign-sounding term when deploring deployments by another government.

"Those who advocate that we unilaterally forego the *modernization* of our forces must prove that this will enhance our security and lead to moderation by the other side —in short, that it will advance, rather than undermine, the preservation of the peace. . . . We will move ahead with our preparations to *modernize* our nuclear forces in Europe. . . . In the United States, we will move forward with the plans I announced last year to *modernize* our strategic nuclear forces, which play so vital a role in maintaining peace by deterring war." (Ronald Reagan, June 9, 1982)

Antonyms: escalation; menacing deployments

See also: *arms control; buildup; deterrence; escalate; modern weapons systems*

modify my position
Antonym: *flip-flop*
See also: *clarify; misspoke*

moneychangers in the temple
Unspecified bad guys with big bucks.
USAGE: If you don't want to name names or ruffle too many corporate feathers, just allude to these biblical baddies and move on.

"There is a glut of oil on the market. The people know there is no shortage. They want to know why this is so and why we would be considering fighting for an oil supply that is not factually correct in the minds of the people, and the people want to know. It is because, in part, the *moneychangers in the temple* are plundering the world's treasuries is what is really involved, and the people want to know." (Representative Robert A. Roe, January 12, 1991)

monopoly
More rarely named as it grows more ubiquitous.

moral base
USAGE: The ambiguity of "moral" renders this a succinct phrase of emphatic ambiguity, with comfort for many and offense for none but devil-worshipers, who do not comprise a sizable proportion of the electorate.

". . . you have to lead from a firm *moral base*." (George Bush, December 5, 1987)

See also: *moral fiber*

moral decay
"We feel that *moral decay* has weakened our country, that it is crippled by a lack of goals and values, and that our public officials have lost faith in us." (Jimmy Carter, July 15, 1976)

See also: *moral erosion*

moral erosion
Summons to mind the dissipation of ethical principles as akin to the loss of topsoil.

See also: *moral fiber*

moral ethic
USAGE: Discuss a "moral ethic" as though it were singular and objective rather than multifaceted and at least some-

what subjective. Pretend that sexual values can and should be uniform.

"Just like the condom campaign, the AIDS education campaign has pointed this Nation down the improper path of discarding a *moral ethic* in public health policy." (Senator Jesse Helms, January 14, 1991)

moral fiber

The metaphysical substance purportedly at the root of domestic conditions.

"Consider, Mr. President, the havoc wrought by a tidal wave of abortion, pornography, incest, illegitimacy, poverty, teenage suicide, AIDS—to name just a few. All have a common thread: A massive breakdown of America's *moral fiber.*" (Senator Jesse Helms, January 14, 1991)

See also: *moral base*

moral imperative

USAGE: When you want to take a position without stepping too hard on some big toes, you might manage to avoid seeming confrontational if you speak about a "moral imperative" that, by implication, renders current policies counterproductive.

"Instead of demanding publicly that Jewish leadership in the U.S. denounce Israel's foreign minister for his justification of Israel's continued close relationship with South Africa, I have been working with Jewish leadership to convince the government of Israel of the *moral imperative* of its extrication from South Africa's apartheid regime." (Representative Charles Rangel, October 12, 1985)

moral leadership
"The Presidency is not merely an administrative office.
That is the least part of it. It is preeminently a place of
moral leadership." (Franklin D. Roosevelt, 1932)

moral stamina
Posits morality as some kind of endurance contestant.
". . . any hope the world has for the survival of peace
and freedom will be determined by whether the American
people have the *moral stamina* and the courage to meet the
challenge of free-world leadership." (Richard M. Nixon,
November 3, 1969)
See also: *wheel of destiny*

moral strength
Often, moral numbness.
"The President's leadership has been superb. His tough-
ness and courage have called upon a *moral strength* in the
Nation which skeptics said no longer existed." (Senator
Jesse Helms, January 12, 1991)

more will than wallet
More desire to seem to want to do something than actually
to do something.
USAGE: This phrase, while hopefully conveying that your
heart is in the right place, can help you to blame budget
constraints whenever you want to block funding for particular purposes.
"The old solution, the old way, was to think that public
money alone could end these problems. But we have
learned that is not so. And in any case, our funds are low.
We have a deficit to bring down. We have *more will than
wallet;* but will is what we need." (George Bush, January 20,
1989)

motivation, our

A multiplicity of motivations described as singular; a hierarchy's motivations depicted as everyone's.

"Historians will not look kindly on what we did in the Vietnam War, though *our motivation* was good." (Senator Paul Simon, May 12, 1991)

move the goalposts

For politicians transfixed with playing games, an ultimate outrage.

"Now that South Africa has achieved the goals Congress set out five years ago, the critics want to *move the goalposts. . . .*" (Representative William S. Broomfield, June 25, 1991)

See also: *level playing field; uneven playing field*

mudslinging

See: *below the belt; cheap shot*

my fellow Americans

A canned portion of instant warmth; just heat and serve.

"*My fellow Americans,* may that ever be our prayer for our country." (Richard M. Nixon, July 28, 1960)

"And so, *my fellow Americans,* ask not what your country can do for you—ask what you can do for your country." (John F. Kennedy, January 20, 1961)

my friends

USAGE: Suitable as an affectionate salutation for large crowds of people, the vast majority of whom you don't have the foggiest acquaintance with.

"And I know, because, *my friends,* I'm a product of that dream. . . . *My friends,* the dream that carried me to this platform is alive tonight. . . . And, *my friends,* if anyone tells you that the American dream . . . But, *my friends,* maintaining the status quo . . . And, *my friends,* what we have done reflects a simple but very profound idea. . . . *My friends,* as president, I'm going to . . . *My friends,* the dream that began in Philadelphia 200 years ago . . . *My friends,* four years from now . . . Yes, *my friends,* it's a time for wonderful new beginnings." (Michael Dukakis, July 21, 1988, speaking to the Democratic National Convention.)

my good friend
In politician-speak, just about any colleague who is not an avowed enemy.
    See also: *friends*

my heart and soul
USAGE: Succinctly offers for public consumption what can only be known privately.
    "The real question, Mr. President, and I mean this with *my heart and soul,* is what kind of message are we sending to the taxpayers back home?" (Senator Jesse Helms, February 28, 1991)

my last press conference
USAGE: Under extreme circumstances, this phrase is a shocker for conveying the finality of your withdrawal from public life. Of course, for every such final decision, the option remains to render it null and void later.
    "You won't have Nixon to kick around anymore, because, gentlemen, this is *my last press conference.*" (Richard M. Nixon, November 7, 1962)

my worthy opponent
My opponent who isn't as worthy as I am.

naked aggression
The worst kind . . . much worse than clothed, especially when the activity is seen as adversely affecting the interests of the United States and its allies.

"Iraq's invasion, dismemberment, and annexation of Kuwait constitute *naked aggression* in its most direct form." (Senator Warren B. Rudman, January 12, 1991)

"I do not subscribe to the view that our interest in freeing Kuwait is purely economic: There is indeed a strong and real moral justification for punishing and deterring *naked aggression*." (Representative John D. Dingell, February 26, 1991)

See also: *unprovoked aggression*

narco-terrorists
See: *drug kingpins; terrorists*

national debt
Proof positive that the nation has been descending into a fiscal hell in a handbasket; a climactic note for a politico-Miltonian (John and Friedman) sermon on frugality lost, reaching its righteous crescendo.

"My fellow Democrats, it's easy enough to create an illusion of prosperity. All you have to do is write hot checks for $200 billion a year. That's what the Reagan-Bush administration has done. That's how they doubled our *national debt* in just seven years." (Senator Lloyd M. Bentsen, July 21, 1988)

See also: *debtor nation*

national defense

National military buildups, extremely lucrative for huge corporations.

"The Texas delegation supports *national defense.* The tradition of Texas believing in a strong defense had to be a factor in these basing decisions." (Senator Phil Gramm, July 1, 1985)

"Democrats want a strong *national defense,* and we'll pay the price to defend freedom." (Senator Lloyd M. Bentsen, July 21, 1988)

See also: *defense spending; modern weapons systems*

national interest, national interests

The vested interests of a powerful few in the nation, writ large over the heads of the public as equivalent to the best interests of the society as a whole.

Usage: A modern equivalent of the royal "we"—"national interest" or "national interests" can be repeated many times, depending on the gravity of the topic; this is usually sufficient to give an impression that you're serious-minded in requisite ways when it comes to foreign policy.

"Concerning the President's press policies . . . I regard my own responsibility in this field as making available to all of you all of the information that I can, consistent with the *national interest,* on as fair and as equitable basis as possible." (Lyndon B. Johnson, March 20, 1965)

"We have a responsibility—to the rest of the world and to our own children—to exert our best efforts of thought and talent and energy to find a solution [to the Vietnam problem]—not an easy solution, for that does not exist; not a quick solution, for that does not exist—but a solution which will preserve our *national interests* without an even wider war in Asia." (Robert F. Kennedy, September 24, 1966)

"The President has dispatched over 400,000 American military personnel to the Persian Gulf to protect the *national interest.* We must support the President in the course he has laid out." (Senator Jesse Helms, January 12, 1991)

"Let it be clear: Our vital *national interests* depend on a stable and secure Gulf." (George Bush, March 6, 1991)

". . . we went in because we had some substantial *national interests* at stake." (Secretary of State James A. Baker III, May 23, 1991, talking about the U.S. government's decision to go to war with Iraq.)

See also: *stability*

national nightmare

Recent events that were difficult, disruptive, traumatic.
USAGE: May as well play into people's hunger for denial and their eagerness to put stark realities behind them, as though deeper and continuing dysfunctions were not involved in recent events.

"My fellow Americans, our long *national nightmare* is over. Our Constitution works. Our great republic is a government of laws and not of men. Here, the people rule." (Gerald R. Ford, August 9, 1974, when sworn in as president.)

national security

USAGE: If you ever choose to broaden the meaning of "national security" to include environmental protection, public health, housing, employment, and social relations, you'll be running counter to the standard usage—which defines U.S. "national security" as primarily applying to such matters as military power, espionage, and geopolitical positioning in various regions of the world.

"When action is required to preserve our *national security,* we will act." (Ronald Reagan, January 20, 1981)

"I say Americans reject completely the philosophy that sells America short, the philosophy that plays politics with our *national security* with loose talk of America's weakness." (Richard M. Nixon, October 1, 1958)

nationalistic

The energies and power of another country that run counter to one's desires.

USAGE: If you don't particularly object to another country's nationalism, call it something else, such as "maturity" or "self-assurance" or "national pride."

"The Japanese, with their *nationalistic* economics policies, successful beyond any other nation in wealth creation and U.S. market control in many sectors, refute the theory of Adam Smith much better than any other critic." (Representative Helen Delich Bentley, 1991)

Antonym: patriotic

naysayers

People who say "nay" when they should be saying "aye-aye."

"The American people consider the source of those charges and look at the record and aren't deceived by the *naysayers.*" (Jimmy Carter, August 23, 1976)

"Of course, there is a role for constructive criticism. But the *naysayers* who deny our national interest, who speak for delay when they really mean never, and who are more interested in narrow political advantage than in the national advantage—there is no room for these if the inner heart and soul of our Nation is to flourish." (Senator Jesse Helms, January 12, 1991)

"Whether it be skeptical allies or domestic political critics, all of the *naysayers* have witnessed President Bush pushing ahead with confidence, energy, and the benefit of a lifetime of military, diplomatic, and political experiences which prepared him for 1991." (Senator Richard G. Lugar, January 17, 1991)

"Finally, and most importantly, to the great American people: The prophets of doom, the *naysayers,* the protesters, and the flag burners all said that you would never stick by us. But we knew better. We knew you would never let us down. By golly, you didn't." (General Norman Schwarzkopf, May 8, 1991)

Antonym: *hope, apostle of*

See also: *doomsayers; prophets of doom; public squabbling*

negotiate
See: *diplomacy*

negotiate in good faith
USAGE: You are always willing to do this, perhaps in sharp contrast to some others.

"We will *negotiate in good faith* and undertake these talks with the same seriousness of purpose that has marked our preparations over the last several months." (Ronald Reagan, June 9, 1982)

neighbor caring for neighbor
USAGE: A wonderful idea that can substitute for government programs to help people. Some heartwarming anecdotes are available as effective accompaniment. Should help to distract from demands that politicians like you actually do something substantial about recurring social problems.

"Isn't it time for us to get personally involved, for our churches and synagogues to restore our spirit of *neighbor caring for neighbor*?" (Ronald Reagan, February 4, 1982)

"And I want to ask you tonight, will you lead our crusade

to restore our tradition of *neighbor caring for neighbor?*" (Ronald Reagan, February 9, 1982)

See also: *caring; points of light, a thousand; voluntarism*

Nervous Nellies
Antiquated.

An LBJ-ism for Americans balking at the Vietnam War.

"There will be some *Nervous Nellies* and some who will become frustrated and bothered and break ranks under the strain. And some will turn on their leaders and on their country and on our fighting men." (Lyndon B. Johnson, May 17, 1966)

See also: *unpatriotic; wimp*

neutralize
Kill.

never announced
A way to imply that something is unknown because it has not been formally acknowledged.

"As far as I know, Israel has *never announced* that it has any nuclear capability." (Secretary of Defense Dick Cheney, May 31, 1991)

never negotiate out of fear . . . never fear to negotiate
No one's going to push us around, but we're always willing to talk.

USAGE: One of the best recyclable couplets from JFK, this saying offers a feathery stroke for hawks and another for doves.

"Let us *never negotiate out of fear*. But let us *never fear to negotiate*." (John F. Kennedy, January 20, 1961)

New American Order
New attempt to invent a cliché, unlikely to catch on in august circles; many at the top of the country's heap like the old American order just fine, thank you.

"The President speaks of the need for a New World Order abroad. This budget speaks to the need for a *New American Order* here at home." (House Budget Committee chair Leon E. Panetta, April 8, 1991)

new beginning
Ascension to higher office, projected as a momentous fresh start for the entire society.

"We face a clear-cut choice this year between the past and the future, between more of the same and a *new beginning*." (Jimmy Carter, October 19, 1976)

"This inauguration ceremony marks a *new beginning*, a new dedication within our Government, and a new spirit among us all." (Jimmy Carter, January 20, 1977)

"All must share in the productive work of this *new beginning*, and all must share in the bounty of a revived economy." (Ronald Reagan, January 20, 1981)

"Yes, my friends, it's a time for wonderful *new beginnings*: a little baby, a new administration, a new era of greatness for America." (Michael Dukakis, July 21, 1988)

See also: *new spirit; renewal*

new conservatism
Much like the old conservatism, but in new bottles.

new liberalism
Much like the old liberalism, but in new bottles.

new spirit

USAGE: Your election to higher office can always be said to evince, or at least coincide with, a "new spirit."

"The passion for freedom is on the rise. Tapping this *new spirit,* there can be no nobler nor more ambitious task for America to undertake on this day of a new beginning than to help shape a just and peaceful world that is truly humane." (Jimmy Carter, January 20, 1977)

See also: *new beginning*

New World Order

As a practical matter, a not-so-new way of giving the world orders. Meet the new boss, more or less the same as the old boss.

"What is at stake is more than one small country; it is a big idea: a *new world order*—where diverse nations are drawn together in common cause, to achieve the universal aspirations of mankind: peace and security, freedom, and the rule of law. Such is a world worthy of our struggle and worthy of our children's future." (George Bush, January 29, 1991)

See also: *rule of law*

nickeling and diming

USAGE: Can make a paucity of funding for certain line items sound stingy, or even Scrooge-like.

"And I think it's important to fund research and development. We've been *nickeling and diming* those research projects." (Senator Wendell H. Ford, August 19, 1990)

no comment

USAGE: When confronted by a reporter's no-win question, there are usually better ways to say no comment than "no comment," which is liable to sound defensive or evasive.

Try other tacks, such as "I'll get back to you." Even "Sorry, but I'm running late" might do in a pinch.

nonbinding
For show.

   See also: *advisory; voluntary guidelines*

no-nonsense
USAGE: Everybody knows that electoral politics is filled with all kinds of nonsense. So a "no-nonsense" description may be helpful even if partly believed, since many people would settle for any reduction in nonsense.

   "[Dukakis] is a take-charge, *no-nonsense* chief executive. . . ." (Democratic National Committee chair Paul G. Kirk, Jr., July 18, 1988)

no provocation
Sometimes, actual provocations denied.

   "This attack had *no provocation* and the whites now understand that they are liable to be attacked in any part of the state where the Indians happen to be in sufficient force. My idea is that, unless removed by the government, they must necessarily be exterminated." (Colorado governor Frederick W. Pitkin, 1879; a rich miner, Pitkin had for many years been part of a successful effort to foment attacks on the Utes—Indians in the Rocky Mountains—as part of a continuous campaign to push them off their land.)

nothing the United States should apologize for
USAGE: When visiting a country brutalized by a regime that was aided by the U.S. government, this phrase may come in handy.

   "There is *nothing the United States should apologize for.*"

(Dan Quayle, March 10, 1990, speaking with reporters on a jet to Chile.)

notion
Usually an idea or viewpoint that one wishes to disparage.

nuclear stockpile, total
Number and combined explosive power of nuclear weapons in the nation's arsenal.
USAGE: A handy sleight-of-tongue phrase that can accurately describe the country's aggregate nuclear weaponry as diminished in size and firepower.

"With regard to nuclear weapons, the simple truth is America's *total nuclear stockpile* has declined. Today we have far fewer nuclear weapons than we had 20 years ago, and in terms of its *total* destructive power, our *nuclear stockpile* is at the lowest level in 25 years." (Ronald Reagan, January 16, 1984)

Caution: Do not utilize in a public setting where someone present might have the knowledge and inclination to respond by pointing out that the dangers of nuclear weapons are not to be found in the numbers or kilotonnage nearly so much as in speed and accuracy—factors that tighten the trip wire for a nuclear exchange by shortening an adversary's response time and heightening fears of a preemptive first strike. Your electoral opponents are highly unlikely to mention that the U.S. arsenal has continuously and dangerously developed long-range speed and accuracy for strategic nuclear missiles such as the Trident, but there is always the hazard that someone at town meetings or other such events might embarrass you by pointing to these factors and deflating your assurances about the "total nuclear stockpile."

See also: *arms control; first-strike weapons; modern weapons systems*

nuclear weapons, elimination of
USAGE: Good verbal cosmetics for putting a smiley face on continuous production of nuclear weapons.

"I have always believed that we should start down the road to the *elimination of nuclear weapons.*" (Ronald Reagan, November 28, 1987)

"We seek the total *elimination* one day *of nuclear weapons* from the face of the Earth." (Ronald Reagan, January 21, 1985)

"And we will move this year a step toward ultimate goal —the *elimination of* all *nuclear weapons* from this Earth." (Jimmy Carter, January 20, 1977)

number one
Dominating the gridiron planet.

"We should all be justly proud of our magnificent victory in the Gulf. And we can honestly say that only America, of all the countries in the world, could have put together the political and military coalitions that made it possible. So, in that sense, we are still the world's *number one* country." (Arkansas governor Bill Clinton, May 6, 1991)

See also: *superpower, only*

Oo Pp

"O" is for Opportunity
"P" is for Pork Barrel

objective standards
Usually subjective standards.

"As a summary argument, I would contend that by all *objective standards* the United States and its allies have moved rapidly to meet aggression in an inaccessible and volatile region of the world and have done so with democratic debate, open media coverage, and substantial sacrifice beyond all reasonable prediction or belief." (Senator Richard G. Lugar, January 17, 1991)

old boy network
USAGE: A good derisive phrase, which may be helpful as you struggle to set yourself up in a new boy network, or perhaps a new boy-girl network.

See also: *incumbent*

oligarchy
Rule by the few over the many.

Warning: Not for describing the governance of the United States. Confine to foreign countries.

open the floodgates
Allow an unstoppable deluge.
USAGE: Summons images of dikes crushed by huge, crashing waves; in some contexts can be mingled with biblical allusions to useful effect, as though urging that apocalypse be prevented.

"[S]ome in the Administration are bowing to the incessant cries of the homosexual rights movement to throw *open the floodgates* which our sensible immigration restrictions have previously kept shut." (Senator Jesse Helms, January 14, 1991)

opportunity

USAGE: This word has the potential to provide quite a buzz for an array of voters with very divergent interests. No one could possibly be against "opportunity"—the political equivalent of a just dessert that promises to be delicious and not fattening. Especially useful for formal speeches, where you won't run the risk of immediate questions as to what kinds of "opportunity," for what people, on what basis, and to what extent.

"In four months, America will elect a new president, and his name will be Michael Dukakis. His theme will be economic *opportunity* for all. . . . The equality of *opportunity* is the ultimate civil right. . . . Of course, we have differences of opinion. But, on the basic issues of justice and *opportunity,* we stand united. Democrats agree that a good job at a fair wage is the passport to *opportunity* in America. . . . the Reagan-Bush administration gave lip service to progress while fighting a frantic, losing battle to turn back the clock on civil rights and equal *opportunity.* . . . every generation of Americans has accepted a responsibility to expand the frontiers of individual *opportunity.* We have expanded that *opportunity.* . . . Taken together and placed in the context of our free-enterprise system, these progressive actions made America the land of *opportunity.* . . . When Michael Dukakis talks about the economics of *opportunity,* he is talking about making our country work again. . . . justice and *opportunity* for all Americans . . . Now that's the American dream that we have nourished and protected for 200 years—the dream of freedom and *opportunity,* the chance for a step up in life. . . . And I want to thank all of you for the *opportunity* to serve America." (Senator Lloyd M. Bentsen, July 21, 1988, speaking to the Democratic National Convention.)

oppression
Elsewhere.

optimist
What every aspiring politician is well advised to be, since downbeat pitches tend not to sell.
USAGE: No matter how appalled you are at present trends, you should proclaim that you're an "optimist."

"It has been the tough-minded *optimists* whom history has proved right in America. It is still true in our time." (Dwight D. Eisenhower, May 20, 1958)

"Somehow or other, *optimist* that I am, I just believe that peace is coming nearer." (Lyndon B. Johnson, September 16, 1964)

"And it's NO fantasy! No indeed, not for people like me, and Ray and Juanita, and Tom and David and many of you in this room, people who—no matter how tough things seem—remain *optimists* because we are the sons and daughters of the giants who refused to believe those who told them it COULDN'T be done, and went ahead and built this miracle of a place—starting in the cities. It COULD be done. It was! Now we have to do it again. Let's do it together!" (New York governor Mario M. Cuomo, August 9, 1991)

Antonym: *doomsayers*
See also: *future, hope for the; hope, apostle of*

ordnance
A sanitized term for bombs and other killing devices.

organized crime
Criminal activities by underworld groups.
USAGE: Rarely applied to criminal activities by large corporations or the government.

orthodoxies, stale
USAGE: The trick is to make your own orthodoxies seem fresh. The buzzphrase "stale orthodoxies" depicts theirs as day-old while yours pop right out of the oven.
   "We've got to have a message that touches everybody, that makes sense to everybody, that goes beyond the *stale orthodoxies* of 'left' and 'right.' " (Arkansas governor Bill Clinton, May 6, 1991)
   See also: *ideologues; ideology; labels*

our allies
By definition, these are countries worth defending.
   "Justice demands that reparations benefit those who suffered and stood up for freedom—American veterans and their families, Kurdish refugees, and *our* Mideast *allies* like Israel and Turkey." (Representative Mel Levine, August 2, 1991)
   "*Our* friends and *allies* in the Middle East recognize that they will bear the bulk of the responsibility for regional security." (George Bush, March 6, 1991)
   Caution: The character of some allied governments should go unmentioned as much as possible, especially when run by torturers, cutthroats, mass murderers, theocrats, etc. If confronted on this point, simply say that "democracy cannot be imposed from afar."
   See also: *moderate*

our argument was not with the people
We may have killed a lot of them, but that wasn't the point.
USAGE: Especially important to repeat this frequently after
a war in order to drum into public consciousness that you
didn't seek to cause human suffering. Instead, the significant result was a victory over the despised leader.

"Before the war started, I made it very clear over and
over again that *our argument was not with the people* of Iraq,
it wasn't even with the regime in Iraq. It was with Saddam
Hussein." (George Bush, July 14, 1991) According to Pentagon estimates, 200,000 Iraqi people were killed during the
war.

our children
USAGE: To top off your testimonials about "our children,"
you'll sometimes want to laud them as "our most valuable
resource."

"No other problem this country faces targets *our children*
so directly—a multinational industry that feeds its greed in
a market of childhood addiction." (Senator Dan Coats,
1989)

See also: *human resources*

out of control
Out of the politician's control.

"In fact, AIDS spending is so far *out of control* that it is
now the only disease which had its own chapter in the committee report." (Senator Jesse Helms, January 14, 1991)

outlaw nation
See: *international law; madman*

owe it to the American people
A magnanimous and selfless verbal aura to festoon one's political intentions.

"I'd *owe it to the American people* to say, 'Hey, I'm up for the job for four more years.' " (George Bush, June 16, 1991)

PACs
Political action committees that give funds to campaigns.
USAGE: If you can't say something bad about PACs publicly, then just take the money and don't say anything at all. However, when expedient, denounce their role in politics; no problem if you've taken PAC money. And, however much you denounce PACs, you'll retain the option of taking their money in the future.

"I think *PACs* have overlived their usefulness." (former senator Paul E. Tsongas, June 15, 1991, after accepting PAC money for campaigns that got him elected to the House of Representatives and the Senate.)

See also: *lobbyists*

partisan
A negative tag for efforts by the opposing party to advance its fortunes.
USAGE: Other politicians' actions, statements, and motivations may be "partisan," but yours never are.

"The American people await action. They didn't send us here to bicker. They ask us to rise above the merely *partisan.*" (George Bush, January 20, 1989)

"The solution of the tremendous social problems of our day should not be a *partisan* affair. . . . America will reach its high destiny only if we remain strongly united. . . ." (Harry S Truman, March 23, 1946)

Antonyms: *bipartisan; country above party*

partisan advantage
USAGE: When trying to gain partisan advantage, consider accusing others of trying to gain partisan advantage.

"I can think of no greater injustice to the men and women of the Armed Forces than to have their needs put aside for the sake of *partisan advantage*." (Senator Jesse Helms, February 6, 1991)

partisan bickering
Any interparty clash lacking approval.

"There's a genuine concern that you not engage the president in *partisan bickering*." (Democratic Party strategist Thomas E. Donilon, December 2, 1990)

"I know there are differences among us about the impact and the effects of a capital gains incentive. So tonight, I am asking the congressional leaders and the Federal Reserve to cooperate with us in a study—led by Chairman Alan Greenspan—to sort out our technical differences so that we can avoid a return to unproductive *partisan bickering*." (George Bush, January 29, 1991)

Antonyms: *bipartisanship; loyal opposition*
See also: *public squabbling*

party unity
In other words, shut up and get with the program.

"In an election campaign *party unity* is essential." (Richard M. Nixon, 1960)

paternalism
Often a disparaging code word for government social programs that aid the poor.
USAGE: If you can get the knack, you may find it convenient to be able to denounce "paternalism" in an authoritatively paternalistic fashion.

"Abroad and at home, the time has come to turn away from the condescending policies of *paternalism*—of 'Washington knows best.' " (Richard M. Nixon, January 20, 1973)

See also: *benign neglect; big government; bleeding heart; welfare*

pathology, tangle of
Derivation: Written by Daniel Patrick Moynihan and released on August 9, 1965, the Moynihan Report proclaimed black families in America to be enmeshed "in a tangle of pathology." The report did not describe prevalent racism or social inequities as any reflection of "pathology" among white people.

patriots
Antonyms: *fanatics; zealots*

Pax Americana
Peace on American terms.
USAGE: That's probably what you want, but no need to say it publicly in so many words. In fact you may want to deny that you have any such thing in mind.

"What kind of peace do I mean? What kind of peace do we seek? Not a *Pax Americana* enforced on the world by American weapons of war." (John F. Kennedy, June 10, 1963)

See also: *peace*

pay-as-you-go
A frugal-sounding notion that tends to put fiscal operation of government on a par with balancing a household checkbook.

"Though controversial, the budget agreement finally put

the federal government on a *pay-as-you-go* plan. . . ." (George Bush, January 29, 1991)

Antonym: *deficit spending*

P.C.
See: *political correctness*

peace
Every politician claims to want it; many politicians make it impossible.

"*Peace* is precious to us. It is the way of life we strive for with all the strength and wisdom we possess. But more precious than *peace* are freedom and justice. We will fight, if fight we must. . . ." (Harry S Truman, January 8, 1951)

"The purpose of our military strength is *peace*. The purpose of our partnership is *peace*." (John F. Kennedy, July 2, 1963)

"Our one desire—our one determination—is that the people of Southeast Asia be left in *peace* to work out their own destinies in their own way." (Lyndon B. Johnson, August 10, 1964)

"Our commitment to strengthening the *peace* has not weakened." (Hubert H. Humphrey, February 17, 1965)

"I do not genuinely believe that there's any single person anywhere in the world that wants *peace* as much as I want it." (Lyndon B. Johnson, May 17, 1966)

"There is no quick and easy way to *peace*—it must and will be built out of the cumulative acts of men and women who dedicate their lives to the service of their fellow men— and therefore to the service of God." (Hubert H. Humphrey, March 1967)

"But our goal is *peace*—and *peace* at the earliest possible moment. . . . I wish—with all of my heart—that the expenditures that are necessary to build and to protect our power could all be devoted to the programs of *peace*. But until world conditions permit, and until *peace* is assured, America's might—and America's bravest sons who wear our Nation's uniform—must continue to stand guard for all of us—as they gallantly do tonight in Vietnam and other places in the world." (Lyndon B. Johnson, January 17, 1968)

peace, preserved the

A happy-face commendation sticker for the U.S. nuclear arsenal.

"With all of the heinous character of the nuclear weapon, it cannot be disinvented. And if one looks back to the troubled conclusion of World War II, it has been that nuclear weapon which has *preserved the peace* over those almost 50 years." (Alexander M. Haig, January 30, 1988)

Caution: Be careful not to use this phrase in front of audiences with large numbers of refugees from recent wars around the world, who may not take kindly to being told that "peace" has been "preserved." Especially inappropriate for elderly Japanese audience.

See also: *arms control*

peace at home

Prevention of domestic upheaval against the status quo.
USAGE: Implies that public tranquillity in the United States is at one with stopping war abroad and that domestic disruptions aimed at warmakers in Washington are necessarily inconsistent with goals of ending war overseas.

"The right to demonstrate for peace abroad does not carry with it the right to break the *peace at home*." (Richard M. Nixon, May 1, 1971)

peace offensive
Activities of peace advocates that war planners find offensive.

peace process
Pretty much whatever process the U.S. State Department is trying to further in international crises. Not to be confused with a process that has peace as its primary goal.

"There's an awful lot of sentiment amongst Palestinians everywhere . . . for this *peace process* to go forward, so let's hope that reason prevails." (George Bush, August 6, 1991)

peace through strength
Military prowess that promises to impose "peace," sooner or later; a.k.a. war is peace.

"Nowhere in the world today is there a clearer road to *peace through strength* than in Vietnam." (Barry Goldwater, 1964)

"In foreign affairs I will continue our policy of *peace through strength*." (George Bush, August 18, 1988)

See also: *deterrence; military preparedness; peace; strength*

peace with honor
USAGE: This phrase became such a chronically repetitive presidential slogan during the Vietnam War that it should be avoided for the foreseeable future.

"We are going to continue to search every day for peace, but a *peace with honor*." (Lyndon B. Johnson, February 2, 1968)

"Let us be proud that by our bold, new initiatives, and by our steadfastness for *peace with honor*, we have made a breakthrough toward creating in the world what the world has not known before—a structure of peace that can last,

not merely for our time, but for generations to come."
(Richard M. Nixon, January 20, 1973)
See also: *New World Order*

peaceful atom
A laudatory term for nuclear power plants as a technology
of benign tranquillity, while avoiding such topics as ever-
present risks of catastrophic reactor accidents and the certainty of nuclear wastes that will remain deadly for many
thousands of years.

Derivation: On December 8, 1953, President Dwight Eisenhower proclaimed a commitment to "atoms for peace"
in a speech to the United Nations: "The United States
pledges before you—and therefore before the world—its
determination to help solve the fearful atomic dilemma—to
devote its entire heart and mind to find the way by which
the miraculous inventiveness of man shall not be dedicated
to his death, but consecrated to his life."

See also: *technological edge*

peaceful revolution
Often a reference to superficial change that won't rock the
boat.

USAGE: A convenient way to claim that one supports the
aspirations of the downtrodden, even while backing many a
regime of downtrodders.

"Those who make *peaceful revolution* impossible will
make violent revolution inevitable." (John F. Kennedy,
March 12, 1962)

"If a *peaceful revolution* is impossible, a violent revolution is inevitable." (Lyndon B. Johnson, October 11, 1964)

peacefully

The meaning is liable to vary according to which side of the big-gun barrels one is on.

"Here, despite occasional conflict, we have *peacefully* shared our hemisphere to a degree unmatched by any nation, anywhere." (Lyndon B. Johnson, March 16, 1964)

"Let me tell you, ma'am, we are trying to resolve this crisis *peacefully*." (Dan Quayle, January 8, 1991, responding to an antiwar protester who had shouted "No war in the Middle East!")

peaceniks

USAGE: If peace demonstrators and the like are causing you trouble, consider calling them names. "Peacenik" is an old standby.

"During a week a short time ago our newspapers, our TV programs and our radio commentators informed us fully about the protesters and the *peaceniks* who invaded the Pentagon. They came there to stay. They walked over the tulips. They sat down on the steps. They slept in the halls." (Lyndon B. Johnson, June 27, 1967)

people, the

Some of the people.

"The lesson of past agony is that without *the people* we can do nothing; with *the people* we can do everything." (Richard M. Nixon, January 20, 1969)

See also: *all Americans; American people, the*

perversion

USAGE: Connotations may vary according to region. In general, whatever sexual activity you would publicly deny ever having done in private.

pessimism

Reprehensibly low Pollyanna quotient.

"One vision sees an America sealed off from the future. . . . It is a vision based on *pessimism,* fear, and self-doubt." (Representative William S. Broomfield, May 23, 1991)

"We have prepared a detailed series of proposals that include: . . . A banking reform plan to bring America's financial system into the 21st century—so that our banks remain safe and secure and can continue to make job-creating loans for our factories, businesses and home-buyers. I do think there has been too much *pessimism.*" (George Bush, January 29, 1991)

"*Pessimism* never won any battle, whether it was in peace or it was in war." (Dwight D. Eisenhower, July 15, 1955)

Antonym: *hope*

See also: *self-doubt*

pet projects

USAGE: Projects that you strongly oppose and some other politicians strongly support.

"It is all too easy for Congress to protect *pet projects* and pork-barrel programs by hiding them in voluminous spending packages." (Representative William S. Broomfield, January 3, 1991)

Antonym: *public works*

See also: *pork barrel*

photo opportunity

Occasion when a politician has invited media cameras. Also known as "photo op."

Caution: The phrase sounds a bit crass and immodest, so leave it to your press aides in public.

piecemeal

USAGE: Keep in mind that you can apply this put-down to almost any programmatic approach you dislike.

"We are forced to rely upon *piecemeal* programs, obsolete policies and meaningless slogans." (John F. Kennedy, June 14, 1960)

piled on

Poli-gridiron talk for being ganged up on.

USAGE: Lacquers self-pity with a thick coat of testosterone.

"I may have set a record for having been *piled on.*" (Senator Charles S. Robb, June 1991)

pitiful helpless giant

The United States failing to flex its muscle.

USAGE: Can suggest a Swiftian image of being tied down by inferior little Lilliputians. Hopefully most people won't notice that this is an extreme hyperbole.

"If when the chips are down, the world's most powerful nation . . . acts like a *pitiful, helpless giant,* the forces of totalitarianism and anarchy will threaten free nations and free institutions throughout the world." (Richard M. Nixon, April 30, 1970, announcing U.S. invasion of Cambodia.)

players

People who count in political games.

pluralism

Toleration, if not acceptance, of diversity.

USAGE: You can give a nod to "pluralism" once in a while without in the least foreclosing your options to demand that ethnic or minority groups steadily give ground in matters of language, customs, and culture.

"*Pluralism* in social services is of course only a part of a larger *pluralism,* ethnic, cultural, and religious, that has made America great and will keep America great." (Jimmy Carter, October 4, 1976)

"If we can bring to our interactions in the world the highest values that we aspire to in our dealings with each other, America can remain a beacon for diverse peoples everywhere—a *pluralistic* society where democracy and a growing economy take all its citizens to a higher ground." (Senator Bill Bradley, April 15, 1991)

See also: *tolerance*

plutocracy

Control of government by the wealthy. For all practical political purposes, a foreign condition only.

Caution: For domestic issues, there's no money behind using this word. And a lot against it.

See also: *oligarchy*

points of light, a thousand

Plenty of private efforts to take care of human needs in the society, so the government can be let off the hook.

". . . a brilliant diversity spread like stars, like *a thousand points of light* in a broad and peaceful sky." (George Bush, August 18, 1988)

"I have spoken of *a thousand points of light,* of all the community organizations that are spread like stars throughout the Nation, doing good." (George Bush, January 20, 1989)

"We can find meaning and reward by serving some purpose higher than ourselves—a shining purpose, the illumination of *a thousand points of light.*" (George Bush, January 29, 1991)

See also: *more will than wallet; neighbor caring for neighbor; voluntarism*

police state
Sometimes a phrase describing government repression; sometimes an absurd attempt to depict constructive government actions as repression.

"This civil rights program about which you have heard so much is a farce and a sham—an effort to set up a *police state* in the guise of liberty. I am opposed to that program. I fought it in Congress. It is the province of the state to run its own elections. I am opposed to the anti-lynching bill because the Federal Government has no more business enacting a law against one kind of murder than another. I am against the FEPC because if a man can tell you whom you must hire, he can tell you whom you cannot employ. I have met this head-on." (Lyndon B. Johnson, May 22, 1948)

policy review
USAGE: When you come to believe that a change in your public stance on an issue would be shrewd, you can say that a "policy review" is under way and your previous position is inoperative.

Antonym: *flip-flop*

political agenda
What certain other people have; never what one has oneself.
USAGE: A rhetorical lever for advancing one's own "political agenda" by accusing others of having one.

"Unfortunately, Mr. President, our efforts to treat AIDS as a public health concern have been thwarted by a vocal, militant minority which has used the AIDS issue to promote a *political agenda* it has failed to achieve in its own right. Of course, I am referring to the homosexual lobby." (Senator Jesse Helms, January 14, 1991)

"I think you've got a *political agenda*." (Senator Ted Stevens, May 1991, denouncing a Smithsonian Institution official for a museum exhibit that reassessed images of America's western frontier history. "To see that exhibit . . . I'll tell you, that really set me off," Stevens said. Actually, he'd never seen the exhibit.)

See also: *social agenda*

political correctness

Politicians and mass media have taken to denouncing attempts to impose "political correctness" (an alleged left-wing dogma with no tolerance for racism or gender inequality). But the politicians and media sounding the loudest alarms often wield enormous clout to define America's politically acceptable boundaries. In effect, "political correctness" is a taunting phrase shouted by the powerful as an accusation against fainter voices trying to get a few words in edgewise. The more that powers-that-be flog the P.C. horse, the more their own hysteria—and intolerance—gain momentum. And along the way, they reinforce the rigorous limits on public discourse already in place.

USAGE: If you want to trash campus activists or anyone else you'd like to silence, accuse them of "political correctness." That way, with two words, you can portray them as trying to do what you've just done—label certain views as beyond the pale of reasonable discussion.

"The notion of *political correctness* has ignited controversy across the land. And although the movement arises from the laudable desire to sweep away the debris of racism and sexism and hatred, it replaces old prejudice with new ones. It declares certain topics off-limits, certain expression off-limits, even certain gestures off-limits." (George Bush, May 4, 1991)

political football
USAGE: When in a nasty conflict, accuse the offending players of using serious issues as a "political football." This, of course, you would never dream of doing; perhaps, for good measure, you are shocked and dismayed to see others stoop so low. Stick to this approach and you're unlikely to fumble the pigskin.

political hay
The rough agricultural equivalent of a "political football."

political prisoners
People incarcerated due to political beliefs and/or actions. American politicians, however, do not apply this term to any such persons inside the United States.
    See also: *human rights*

political unparticipants
People who don't see any point in voting.

political will
Not to be confused with a dying politician's bequest, this is a term for what opponents lack by way of determination to achieve a particular goal.
USAGE: Implies that political change is an est-like process impeded not by real power-bloc obstacles but rather by insufficient psychological fortitude.

politics as usual
As usual, part of a promise to be different from the usual.
    "Nineteen seventy-six will not be a year of *politics as usual.* It can be a year of inspiration and hope. . . ." (Jimmy Carter, July 15, 1976)

"At my age I didn't go to Washington to play *politics as usual.*" (Ronald Reagan, October 29, 1982)

pollsters
USAGE: In public, pretend to be unconcerned with the findings of "pollsters."

See also: *fashionable*

poor excuses for Americans
Poor excuse for civil discourse.

"What we cannot be proud of, Mr. Speaker, is the unshaven, shaggy-haired, drug culture, *poor excuses for Americans . . .*" (Representative Gerald B. H. Solomon, January 17, 1991)

See also: *blame-America-first crowd*

pork barrel
Some verbal lard to throw at opposed appropriations.

"The dole is dead. The *pork barrel* is gone." (Lyndon B. Johnson, March 9, 1965)

"They'll use the money on more *pork barrel* projects and other wasteful spending." (Representative Fred Upton, June 25, 1991)

Antonym: *public works*

See also: *pet projects*

pornography
USAGE: If you choose to denounce "pornography," you will probably not want to provoke fears that you seek to deprive people of magazines such as *Playboy, Penthouse,* etc. As a practical matter, it is best to give voters the impression that what you oppose is only the "pornography" that is decidedly more hard-core and extreme than the licentious material they are currently enjoying.

power

USAGE: Publicly your aims are to contain ominous forces while using "power"—with reluctance, not eagerness. So refer to power in that context. Lapses, as in the oft-quoted moment of candor by Henry Kissinger, are apt to be quickly noted and long remembered.

"The exercise of *power* in this century has meant for all of us in the United States not arrogance but agony. We have used our *power* not willingly and recklessly ever, but always reluctantly and with restraint." (Lyndon B. Johnson, May 11, 1966)

"Our 'doves' must learn that there are times when *power* must be used. They must learn that there is no substitute for force in the face of a determined enemy who resorts to terror, subversion and aggression, whether concealed or open." (Hubert H. Humphrey, June 8, 1966)

"*Power* is the great aphrodisiac." (Henry A. Kissinger, January 19, 1971.)

power brokers

Sometimes reviled, but much more often consulted.

"This has been a long and personal campaign—a humbling experience, reminding us that ultimate political influence rests not with the *power brokers* but with the people." (Jimmy Carter, 1976)

See also: *back room; smoke-filled rooms*

pragmatic

In many cases, making a virtue out of necessity.

USAGE: If you ditch formerly proclaimed principles, tell anyone who gives you a hard time that you have to be "pragmatic." You might try some sighing, too.

pragmatism
Antonyms: *appeasement; caving in*
See also: *realism*

pray
USAGE: Whether you do or not, say you do. Never, never, never say you don't.

prayer, never forget the power of
USAGE: Never forget the rhetorical power of telling an audience never to forget the power of prayer.

prayer in schools
USAGE: Depending on the constituency, the absence of school prayer can be depicted as the root of much evil over the past three decades.

"The American people understand that the abandonment of principles and values was in large part due to a series of decisions by unelected, elitist liberals on the [U.S.] Supreme Court who, in 1962, outlawed *prayer in public schools.*" (Senator Jesse Helms, January 14, 1991)

"The right to *pray in school* is a fundamental American liberty." (Ronald Reagan, February 6, 1986)

See also: *intolerance of Christianity*

prayers
USAGE: Never hurts to ask for them. Hopefully votes will follow along later.

"My fellow Americans, I once asked you for your *prayers,* and now I give you mine. May God guide this wonderful country. . . ." (Gerald R. Ford, January 12, 1977)

"To my constituents in California, I thank you as well for your opinions, your thoughts, and your *prayers.*" (Senator John Seymour, January 12, 1991)

President, Mr.
A form of address that is both salutation and genuflection.

presidential, very
USAGE: If you want to praise a speech by the president but can't think of anything else to say.

pressure group
A group exerting unappreciated pressure.

"I can assure you if I am elected President that Walter Reuther, or no other leader of labor, business or any other group in our country will have a key to the back door or even the side door of the White House. The American people had enough of that kind of *pressure group* dictation in the years before 1953. They don't want any part of it now." (Richard M. Nixon, November 3, 1960)

    Antonym: *constituents*
    See also: *special interests*

principle, matter of
A phrase of self-praise, ideal for making a bigger virtue out of virtue.

private sector
A rosy moniker that puts megacorporations in the same "sector" as small, family-owned businesses.

privilege
Often a right that is being used in a way one doesn't like. Can make the First Amendment sound revocable, like a driver's license.
USAGE: Implies that irresponsible people might not deserve such rights after all.

"Political extremists roam the land, abusing the *privilege* of free speech, setting citizens against one another on the basis of their class or race." (George Bush, May 4, 1991)

". . . we recognize that it's a *privilege,* not a right, to work for the government and that we should remove from the payroll those of doubtful loyalty and those who might be easy prey to espionage agents because of their personal habits or their backgrounds." (Richard M. Nixon, March 15, 1954)

"To work for the U.S. Government is a *privilege,* not a right. And it is the prerogative of the government to set the strictest test upon the loyalty and the patriotism of those entrusted with our nation's safety." (Dwight D. Eisenhower, October 3, 1952)

See also: *behavior; responsibility*

proabortion

USAGE: If your position is that abortion should be outlawed, call those with the opposite view "proabortion." In that way you can portray them as championing abortions rather than supporting a woman's right to choose whether to have an abortion.

prodemocracy

A highly selective term for certain advocates of democratization in certain countries. Therefore, activists for democratic change inside Communist nations have been called "prodemocracy" by many U.S. politicians. But activists for democratic change elsewhere—blacks in South Africa, for instance, or Palestinians in the occupied territories of the West Bank and Gaza, or student demonstrators in South Korea—are not graced with the "prodemocracy" label.

productivity

USAGE: Remember that while it can be politic to blame lagging U.S. productivity on a number of factors, high military spending is usually not one of them. So stay in formation, don't ask for trouble, and—even when lauding the superior pace of economic growth in Japan and Germany—avoid emphasizing that those countries have minuscule military budgets compared to the Pentagon.

"Government can and must provide opportunity, not smother it; foster *productivity,* not stifle it." (Ronald Reagan, January 20, 1981)

"Our competitors for the future are Germany and Japan. Last year they had *productivity* growth rates three and four times ours because they educate their people better, they invest more in their future, and they organize their economies for global competition and we don't." (Arkansas governor Bill Clinton, May 6, 1991)

See also: *individual initiative*

pro-family

USAGE: Anyone who objects to what is proposed under a "pro-family" rubric can be depicted, at least by innuendo, as anti-family.

". . . now is the time to fire the engines of growth with tax reform that is pro-fairness, *pro-family,* and pro-future." (Ronald Reagan, February 6, 1986)

"These principles have guided my efforts in the past. And now they will provide the foundation for legislation I will introduce next week in the Senate—a package of 25 *pro-family* bills we intend to call the American Family Act." (Senator Dan Coats, 1989)

See also: *American family, the; family; values, family*

pro-growth

Growth for growth's sake is the ideology of the cancer cell.
USAGE: Growth, of course, is inevitable, and many issues
boil down to what kind of growth. By proclaiming a "pro-
growth" outlook, however, you can imply that opponents
are inexplicably opposed to progress and prosperity.

"Democrats must be aggressively pro-jobs, *pro-growth,*
pro-competitiveness and pro-business." (former senator
Paul E. Tsongas, June 22, 1991)

pro-life

A common self-description by those who want to ban abortions.
USAGE: A way to declare that people who do not want to
ban abortions are anti-life.

promises, broken

See: *bankrupt policies; incumbent*

propaganda

Expression of repugnant viewpoints. Propaganda other
than one's own and that of one's allies.

"We should listen more carefully to popular music, because at its best it is worthy of more serious appreciation,
and at its worst it is blatant drug-culture *propaganda.*"
(Spiro Agnew, September 14, 1970)

prophets of doom

USAGE: Dire predictions that contradict your upbeat scenarios can be ascribed to dour "prophets of doom."

". . . I am convinced that the complainers in this country and the critics in this country and the *prophets of doom*
in this country and the fear artists in this country are very,

very much in the minority." (Lyndon B. Johnson, October 13, 1966)

"But for me, the echo of the campaign of 1984 rang louder than the *prophets of doom*." (Democratic National Committee chair Paul G. Kirk, Jr., July 18, 1988)

Caution: In written statements, do not mistake for "prof-its of doom."

Antonym: *hope, apostle of*

See also: *doomsayers; naysayers*

prophylactic segregation

Quarantine.

[Q.: Would you support quarantines of those infected with AIDS?] "It's very clear to me that there are some categories which are going to require mandatory testing. And rather than use the word 'quarantine' I'd prefer to use *'prophylactic segregation.'* . . ." [Q.: Just what is the differ-ence between quarantine and prophylactic segregation?] "Well, there is really none. It's just the term quarantine sometimes connotes a sort of a forced isolation that is sometimes distasteful to those who really would at the same time prefer to be protected from an innocent acquisition of the virus." (Alexander M. Haig, January 30, 1988)

See also: *innocent Americans; innocent victims of AIDS*

protectionism

USAGE: Sounds bad—so if you're in favor of initiating trade wars and putting up lots of trade barriers, go out of your way to insist that what you're urging is absolutely not "pro-tectionism." Talk instead about "fair play."

See also: *good-faith effort; level playing field*

public cynicism
Skepticism, usually warranted; an unwillingness to believe government officials who have repeatedly proven themselves untrustworthy.

"Democracy itself cannot indefinitely survive *public cynicism* and contempt." (Representative Henry J. Hyde, November 29, 1990)

See also: *crisis of confidence*

public interest, the
Rhetorical fabric that can be cut to clothe any politician's personal interest.

"The continuing headlines and speculation based on comments from anonymous sources may provide entertainment for readers and viewers. But it is appalling to anyone who cares about the Commonwealth [of Virginia] and the gains made by a proud political party during the last decade. I am personally committed to put an end to it. I believe *the public interest* demands it." (Senator Charles S. Robb, June 1991)

public outrage
The facets of widespread anger that a politician chooses to acknowledge.

public servant
Politician, often self-serving.

"I am just a *public servant* that is doing the very best I know how." (Lyndon B. Johnson, March 25, 1964)

public service
Activities that run the gamut from sincere efforts at social betterment to narcissistic and sustained binges of power mania. Often a pleasant euphemism for political ambition.

"It's basically a struggle between personal factors that say no and the *public service* side that says yes." (George S. McGovern, May 1991, describing his dilemma about whether to run for president.)

"And we want to bring back to Washington people who are more interested in *public service* than they are in private gain." (Jimmy Carter, July 18, 1988)

"It is all too easy for the government official . . . to forget that ours is a government FOR the people and that those in government are in *public service,* not self-service." (Hubert H. Humphrey, December 8, 1965)

public squabbling
Expressions of dissent from prevailing policy.

"When U.S. troops are sent abroad in defense of the Nation against specific challenges to our national sovereignty and independence, this Senator believes that the issues involved are too important for *public squabbling.*" (Senator Jesse Helms, January 12, 1991)

Antonym: *bipartisanship*
See also: *naysayers; partisan bickering*

public works
Projects close to home.

Antonyms: *pet projects; pork barrel*

pushed us over the line
USAGE: Handy for presenting complex situations as matters of pride. Also good for making the issue personal, so people will feel that the villain has made a personal challenge to each and every one of us.

"He must know he has *pushed us over the line* and that his insistence on the occupation of Kuwait and the threat against Saudi Arabia is an extreme act of provocation that would be met with force." (Jesse Jackson, August 3, 1990)

put aside our differences
Defer to expediency.

"As Americans, we share the goal of freeing Kuwait from its Iraqi occupiers. Some of us have differed on the means to achieve that goal, but now that military action has begun, we must *put aside our differences* and pray for a swift, successful end to hostilities, with as few casualties as possible." (Senator Paul Simon, January 24, 1991)

Qq Rr

"Q" is for Quotas
"R" is for Revenue Enhancement

quotas
Negative buzzword used to attack a wide range of laws and programs for beginning to rectify centuries of bias that have favored (and continue to favor) whites and males to the detriment of other people.

USAGE: Crank it up. "Quotas" sound bad, so blur the issues as much as possible, say you're for "civil rights," "equal opportunity," and the like, but against affirmative action programs, which you can slam by calling them "quotas." In that way you'll appeal to white racists as well as many whites who mean well but are susceptible to having their buttons pushed, especially because of their own economic frustrations. This is a "wedge issue" whose time has come

—so drive the wedge, and hopefully you'll induce a lot of white people to pull the lever for you.

"In looking over this legislation there are several surprises which will oblige senators to choose between an America stratified by racial and ethnic *quotas,* an America whose law codifies a system where benefits and advantages are doled out according to group identity—or an America where citizens advance through individual initiative and excellence." (Senator Jesse Helms, February 26, 1991)

"Yet the supporters of the new Civil Rights Act want to go far beyond reasonable guarantees. They would rather institute new hiring *quotas* and open the door to unlimited compensatory and punitive damage claims." (Representative Bill Dickinson, May 1991)

"I'm the kind of Democrat who's against racial discrimination and against racial *quotas.* I marched from Selma to Montgomery in the rain and mud with Martin Luther King because I believed then and I believe now in his dream of an America where all of us will be judged 'by the content of our character, not the color of our skin.' And when I was a college president and students took over my office demanding racial *quotas* I said no that's wrong; I said that's not what civil rights is all about. And you know who stood with me? Most of the black students at that school, who wanted a good, hard education, leading to good, solid jobs. They wanted equal opportunity, not *quotas.*" (Senator Harris Wofford, June 1, 1991)

Synonyms: *reverse discrimination; unfair preferences*
See also: *color-conscious; two choices*

rabid environmentalists

People trying to prevent ecological damage—portrayed as dirty dogs foaming at the mouth, and blamed for all sorts of events actually manipulated by (purportedly sane) anti-environmentalists.

"The greenies have led us into the crisis in the Middle East. . . . The *rabid environmentalists* felt it was more important to jeopardize the lives of our brave American servicemen than risk the death of a single snail darter." (Representative Tom DeLay, November 3, 1990)

See also: *greenies; two choices*

radical
Outside sanctioned political boundaries.

"*Radicals* of the right and *radicals* of the left are a small minority in the nation. But their influence is far greater than their number because they are so active and noisy." (Richard M. Nixon, October 1962)

Synonym: *militant*
Antonyms: *moderate; responsible*

rape
A chronic epidemic in the United States, where well-designed studies calculate that up to one third of females will be raped at some time (mostly by men who are not strangers to them). Politicians, however, like to use this word only in two contexts: (1) rhetoric to support "anticrime" legislation with the effect of eroding protections of the Bill of Rights (see also: *afraid to walk the streets; rapists*), or (2) apoplectic verbiage about the "rape" of one country by another, although the metaphor is never applied to U.S. attacks on other countries.
USAGE: Whatever the context, this word should be uttered with a maximum of repugnance, outrage, and exhortation for just retribution.

"So both moral principle and practical politics present compelling reasons to favor the reversal of Saddam Hussein's murderous and violent *rape* of Kuwait." (Senator John Seymour, January 12, 1991)

rapists

USAGE: The specter of rapists walking the streets is a time-worn way of boosting favored legislation when it's objectionable on civil liberties grounds.

"Let me assure you and the people of California that I will have no patience when it comes to the thieves, thugs, *rapists,* killers and drug-runners who prey on innocents in California." (California governor Pete Wilson, January 10, 1991)

"The only real question before the Senate is, do we let the evidence in at trial, or do we let the murderers, robbers, *rapists* and drug dealers go free?" (Senator Orrin G. Hatch, June 25, 1991)

"Senator Mitchell ought to go out and talk to the 6,500 families who were murder victims in the last 100 days. He ought to talk to the 40,500 women who were *raped.*" (Representative Newt Gingrich, June 11, 1991)

Caution: Do not allude to the fact that every year, in effect, millions of Americans rape their children or young relatives in the privacy of their own homes, without governmental interference. Citizens who much prefer to deny that these rapists exist in large numbers are a major portion of the voting public.

See also: *two choices*

read my lips
Do we have to?

"And all I can say to them: *Read my lips*—no new taxes." (George Bush, August 18, 1988)

realism
Synonym: cold, hard facts
  Antonym: *bean counting*

recovery, economic
Often heralded by politicians, describing a phantom that many millions of Americans never see for themselves.

recycled paper, printed on
USAGE: If constituents receiving your newsletters tend to be environmentalists, you may want to add, "with soy ink."

red tape
Everybody hates it.
USAGE: You can't go wrong by vowing to cut through it.
  See also: *big government; bureaucracy*

Red tide
Obsolete.
  "We retain a geographical advantage, essential to adequate dispersal and warning systems, and to the encouragement of local resistance to the *Red tide*." (John F. Kennedy, August 14, 1958)

Reds
Obsolete (except in Cincinnati area, and among baseball fans generally).

reevaluation
See: *policy review*

reforms
Sounds good. Can mean just about anything: real or imagined change, constructive or not.

"My plan *reforms* our government to produce new ways to do the important jobs of education, criminal justice and mental health." (New York governor Mario M. Cuomo, February 13, 1991)

regressive taxation

When tax burden falls as income rises. Often disguised as "tax reform."

regulations, vast web of

Uncle Sam cast as Spider-Man.

"Over the past decade the government has spun a *vast web of regulations* that intrude into almost every aspect of every American's working day." (Ronald Reagan, February 10, 1982)

regulatory hoops

A put-down applicable to any and every legal requirement, no matter how beneficial for the general public.

"Mr. Speaker, as we return home for the August recess, we will all have the opportunity to meet and talk with the small-business owners in our districts. We need to hear about the *regulatory hoops* they are forced to jump through for OSHA, IRS, EPA, and the whole alphabet soup of federal agencies who claim authority over their business affairs." (Representative Andy Ireland, August 1, 1991)

rejectionism

Refusal to go along with the type of political settlement favored by the White House in international disputes, particularly conflicts between Palestinians and the Israeli government.

USAGE: When Israel refuses to consider the idea of a Palestinian state, don't call this "rejectionism." Only use the pejorative against Arabs.

reliance on Mideast oil
USAGE: Although only a small percentage of oil consumed in the United States comes from the Middle East, this phrase can give a boost to any number of polemical objectives. Whether you're trying to promote military intervention in that region, offshore oil drilling at home, energy conservation or mass transit, the myth of U.S. "reliance" on Mideast oil is one you'll want to perpetuate as useful. The big oil companies and arms manufacturers will be appreciative.

"As he prepares a national energy policy—a policy desperately needed given our *reliance on Mideast oil*—President Bush has unveiled a budget containing a 36 percent reduction in energy conservation grants and research." (Senator Tom Harkin, February 4, 1991)

Synonyms: dependence on foreign oil; dependence on Mideast oil; reliance on foreign oil

religious leaders
USAGE: When you can marshal support for your policy positions from "religious leaders," hold high-profile meetings with them and laud their wisdom. When you can't, ignore them as much as possible.

religious people, a
USAGE: Often interchangeable with good, ethical, moral.

"We are *a religious people*." (Jimmy Carter, July 18, 1988)

"We are essentially *a religious people*." (Dwight D. Eisenhower, August 19, 1954)

renewal

USAGE: "Renewal" has a variety of connotations, ranging from mild convenience to delirious transcendence. People are likely to associate the word with the implication they're most comfortable with; certain persons will think of getting more time for library books or extending a driver's license; others will picture some kind of humanistic recharging; still others will think of blood, wine, wafers, holy ghosts, stones rolling away from caves, and the like. This is one of those fine pliant words you can use with assurance; like some sort of spandex material, the word's fabric can be supple and snappy enough to assure a snug fit.

"We observe today not a victory of party, but a celebration of freedom—symbolizing an end, as well as a beginning—signifying *renewal,* as well as change." (John F. Kennedy, January 20, 1961)

"So, with all the creative energy at our command, let us begin an era of national *renewal.*" (Ronald Reagan, January 20, 1981)

"We have within our reach the promise of a *renewed* America." (George Bush, January 29, 1991)

"Our Persian Gulf troops . . . have made us prouder than ever to be Americans—and I believe that they are sending us a message that cannot be ignored. I believe our troops are telling us that we must not allow a great *renewal* of the American spirit to begin and end on foreign shores." (Senator Wendell H. Ford, June 22, 1991)

Antonym: *decline*

See also: *new beginning*

renewal, urban

Increasingly, gentrification and realty speculation that means big profits for some investors and unaffordable housing for many urban renewees—details rarely addressed when politicians advocate "urban renewal."

reopen old wounds
Disrupt denial.
USAGE: With this imagery you can portray people confronting social injuries as vindictive troublemakers.

"So let us reject any among us who seek to *reopen old wounds* and to rekindle old hatreds. They stand in the way of a seeking nation." (Lyndon B. Johnson, January 20, 1965)

resistance, the
USAGE: Has a World War II echo, perhaps evoking Bogart in a French seaport. So whenever you support any military insurgency anywhere, whatever the circumstances, you may as well call it "the resistance."

resolve
Credible indication of willingness to go to war, and perhaps to incinerate the planet with nuclear weapons. It's a bird; it's a plane; it's Machomannnnnn!

"America's deterrence is more credible, and it is making the world a safer place—safer because now there is less danger that the Soviet leadership will underestimate our strength or question our *resolve*." (Ronald Reagan, January 16, 1984)

". . . 45 postwar years of American military preparedness and national *resolve*." (Senator Dan Coats, 1990)

"There should be no doubt as to the justness of our cause or the firmness of our *resolve*." (Senator Daniel K. Inouye, January 12, 1991)

"If we had failed to authorize the use of force in the Persian Gulf, Iraq's bold gamble would have paid off. Saddam Hussein would have been able to wait for the inevitable fracturing of the allied coalition. Our partners in that coalition, seeing a lack of American *resolve,* would inevitably have begun to cut their deals with Saddam Hussein." (Senator Alfonse M. D'Amato, January 12, 1991)

"If we maintain our *resolve* and our momentum, we have an important historical opportunity to help establish and maintain a global system of peaceful security." (Senator Richard G. Lugar, January 17, 1991)

See also: *deterrence; military preparedness*

respect for authority
Often, fear of authority.

responsibility
Often juxtaposed with rights or opportunities, as a way to inculcate the idea that government giveth them and can taketh them away unless a quid pro quo—"responsibility" —is forthcoming from particular citizens.
USAGE: Dating back to school days, people are accustomed to lectures on responsibility. "Rights and responsibilities" is a phrase that can fruitfully re-create tensions and memories of submission to authority. Government can be described as ideally giving rights and opportunities rather than assuring them. What matters here is that you must walk a careful wavy line, conveying that people have rights but must prove that they deserve access to them in the future.

"And today, as never before in the free world, *responsibility* is the greatest right of citizenship and service is the greatest of freedom's privileges." (Robert F. Kennedy, September 29, 1962)

"Our privileges can be no greater than our obligations. The protection of our rights can endure no longer than the performance of our *responsibilities.*" (John F. Kennedy, 1963)

"Let us remember that America was built not by government, but by people—not by welfare, but by work—not by shirking *responsibility,* but by seeking *responsibility.*" (Richard M. Nixon, January 20, 1973)

"Moreover, by failing to promote self, family, and community *responsibility,* these programs encourage dependency and entrench the very poverty they were intended to alleviate." (Ronald Reagan, February 6, 1986)

"An effective government must know its limitations and respect its people's capabilities. In return, people must assume the final burden of freedom—and that's *responsibility.*" (George Bush, May 4, 1991)

"But opportunity for all is not enough. For if we give opportunity without insisting on *responsibility,* much of the money can be wasted and the country's strength can still be sapped. So we favor *responsibility* for all. That's the idea behind national service. It's the idea behind welfare reform. . . . *Responsibility* for all means that students ought not get or keep their driver's licenses unless they stay in school. . . . The Democrats should be for *responsibility* for all." (Arkansas governor Bill Clinton, May 6, 1991)

See also: *behavior; privilege*

responsible
Staying in line. Functioning in accordance with U.S. governmental priorities.

"I have never discussed with a human being something he should say or shouldn't say on Vietnam. I think debate's healthy. It's good for us, provided it's *responsible.*" (Lyndon B. Johnson, March 20, 1965)

Synonym: *moderate*
Antonyms: *militant; radical*

restraint

No matter how murderous and continuous a military on-slaught may be, those who order and support it are apt to describe it as "restraint," on the theory that it could be worse.

"And the other side must not take advantage of our *restraint* as they have in the past. This Nation simply cannot accept anything less without jeopardizing the lives of our men and of our allies." (Lyndon B. Johnson, January 17, 1968)

"The history of our era has taught us that peace is best preserved through strength—strength used with *restraint*, with wisdom, and with a clear sense of perspective." (Hubert H. Humphrey, October 24, 1964)

"Let the record show that our *restraint* is not inexhaustible." (John F. Kennedy, April 20, 1961)

restrictions on the economy

USAGE: A handy pejorative for any tax structure or regulatory apparatus you oppose.

"The greatest part of our economic program that we implemented in 1981, my first year here . . . were tax cuts. But the tax cuts [resulted] in more revenue for the government because we lifted *restrictions on the economy* by lowering those high taxes and so forth." (Ronald Reagan, November 28, 1987)

See also: *economic barriers*

revenue enhancement

Taxes by any other name.

USAGE: If you need this linguistic deus ex machina to airlift you out of a tight political corner, don't hesitate to scurry aboard. Remember, no politician has ever promised, "Read my lips: No new revenue enhancement."

reverse discrimination
See: *color-conscious; quotas*

rhetoric
Flowery or emphatic utterances one dislikes.

USAGE: To denounce the "rhetoric" of adversaries effectively, you will need to summon appreciable rhetorical skills.

"In these difficult years, America has suffered from a fever of words; from inflated *rhetoric* that promises more than it can deliver; from angry *rhetoric* that fans discontents into hatreds; from bombastic *rhetoric* that postures instead of persuading." (Richard M. Nixon, January 20, 1969)

"Nor could they find it in their hearts to match their own *rhetoric*. They talked of 'fiscal responsibility.' But the Republican Party borrowed selfishly from your future. . . ." (Democratic National Committee chair Paul G. Kirk, Jr., July 18, 1988)

"My friends, America has just passed through the ultimate epoch of illusion: An eight-year coma in which slogans were confused with solutions, and *rhetoric* passed for reality. . . ." (Senator Lloyd M. Bentsen, July 21, 1988)

rhetoric, empty
Rhetoric presumably inferior to the full-blown variety.

right-to-life
See: *pro-life*

right-wing
To some minds a pejorative.
Antonym: *left-wing*

rising tide will lift all boats, a
The richly encouraged idea that if the rich keep getting richer, everyone else will benefit too. While it doesn't hold water, literally or otherwise, this is a pithy metaphorical rationalization for fiscal policies that favor the wealthy, who are most helpful filling campaign coffers.

"So this isn't trickle down; this is *a rising tide* that *will lift all boats.*" (Representative Jack Kemp, December 19, 1987)

rough-and-tumble
Hard-fought, not dirty fighting.
    Antonym: *below the belt*
    See also: *dirty tricks*

rule of law
When those who made the rules lay down the law.

"It is a victory for the *rule of law* and for what is right. Desert Storm's success belongs to . . ." (George Bush, March 6, 1991)

"We go on record again today, in hope that this remarkable international coalition effort will dissuade future aggressors from adopting the ill-fated policies of Saddam Hussein. Hopefully, these actions will serve to establish the *rule of law* among all nations and the peoples of those nations." (Representative Dante Fascell, March 5, 1991)

"Where Saddam Hussein trampled on the *rule of law,* you must uphold it." (Dan Quayle, February 26, 1991, speaking to 263 Kuwaiti soldiers at Fort Dix, New Jersey.)

"There are those who complain of the loss of sovereignty involved in membership in the United Nations, or in the Organization of American States, or in NATO, or in signing any international treaty. But without the *rule of law,* the rule of the jungle prevails." (Hubert H. Humphrey, January 6, 1967)

"I believe it would be a grave mistake to charge off the recent riots to unredressed Negro grievances alone. To do so is to ignore a prime reason and a major national problem: the deterioration of respect for the *rule of law* all across America." (Richard M. Nixon, August 15, 1966)

See also: *international law; New World Order*

rumor and insinuation

Allegations that haven't been proven—yet.

USAGE: Accompany with a tone of rising indignation.

"I just don't think it's the American way to bring a good man down by *rumor and insinuation*." (George Bush, July 12, 1991, speaking of his nominee to head the CIA, Robert Gates.)

Synonym: rumor and innuendo
Antonym: *smoking gun*
See also: *fair play*

runaway spending

USAGE: Can evoke images of the governmental engine careening down steep inclines toward cataclysm, while you endeavor to grab the steering wheel and slam on the brakes.

See also: *out of control; tax and spend*

ruthlessness

Depravity both cruel and without redeeming utility.

USAGE: To be ascribed to brutal American adversaries, though not to brutal American allies.

"In Saddam Hussein we confront an imperial dictator whose ambitions are surpassed only by the *ruthlessness* with which they are pursued." (Senator Warren B. Rudman, January 12, 1991)

"Nevertheless, I know of no thinking human being who

does not understand the economic importance of that region of the world, and the fact that the energy security of the U.S. and the world is at risk from the threat of a *ruthless* scoundrel such as Saddam Hussein." (Representative John D. Dingell, February 26, 1991)

Ss Tt

"S" is for Soak-the-Rich Schemes
"T" is for Tax and Spend

sacrifices
Usually the real or exaggerated burdens shouldered by some to implement policies that end up aggrandizing others.

"On the *sacrifices* of men who died for their country and their comrades, our freedom has been built." (Lyndon B. Johnson, April 21, 1966)

"So, together, in a spirit of individual *sacrifice* for the common good, we must simply do our best." (Jimmy Carter, January 20, 1977)

"A national effort, entailing *sacrifices* by the American people, is now under way to make long-overdue improvements in our military posture." (Ronald Reagan, June 9, 1982)

"I believe that the Desert Shield and Desert Storm experiences have forced us to confront questions about our role in the world and to understand the potential risks and *sacrifices* involved in being the leader." (Senator Richard G. Lugar, January 17, 1991)

"On the other hand, there was bound to be opposition to

such a complex and demanding package. It has come from a variety of individual interest groups that have insisted that they be exempted from any *sacrifice*." (New York governor Mario M. Cuomo, February 13, 1991)

Saddam
A modern-day companion for Gomorrah.

safety
Often a delusionary term for a situation in which the more dangerous the preparations are, the more "safety" is said to exist, as in the case of arsenals bristling with weapons of mass destruction.

USAGE: Since people so often confuse words with realities, the reiteration of "safety" makes many people feel safer.

"I happen to think our Defense Department ought to have a margin of *safety* for our national security. The question is how you achieve that margin of *safety*. It's my judgment that the present level of defense appropriations is about right." (Gerald R. Ford, November 28, 1987)

See also: *defense; national security*

safety net
Increasingly, a thin weave of social services with big holes.

sanctity of human life
USAGE: Of course, you don't mean ALL human life.

"National *Sanctity of Human Life* Day" (proclaimed by President Bush, January 20, 1991, a few days after ordering the U.S. attack on Iraq.)

secret plan
USAGE: When you can insist that it must be kept confidential for "national security" reasons, you might want to say

that you have a "secret plan" to solve an especially intracta-
ble international crisis. (Richard Nixon found that enough
people were gullible for him to pull this off during the 1968
presidential race, when he announced that he had a "secret
plan" to end the Vietnam War. Two decades later, Nixon
admitted he had no such plan, and acknowledged it was
merely a campaign ploy.) After all, it's hard for opponents
to criticize a phantom plan—and if they ever demand details, you can blast them for failure to comprehend the exigencies of maintaining diplomatic secrecy in such matters.

secure the peace

"Our friends and allies in the Middle East recognize that
they will bear the bulk of the responsibility for regional
security. But we want them to know that just as we stood
with them to repel aggression so now America stands ready
to work with them to *secure the peace.*" (George Bush,
March 6, 1991)

See: *win the peace*

security

Security for some, temporarily.

USAGE: You can follow "security" with any number of words
—arrangements, assistance, burdens, interests, measures,
provisions—and define them more or less as you please.

"*Security* based upon heavy armaments is a way of life
that has been forced upon us and upon our Allies. We don't
like it; in fact, we hate it. But so long as such an unmistak-
able, self-confirmed threat to our freedom exists, we will
carry these burdens with dedication and determination."
(Dwight D. Eisenhower, April 30, 1953)

"We must retain the armed strength needed for *security*
in a troubled world, but we should speak with the calm

assurance of those who are not afraid." (Richard M. Nixon, November 26, 1958)

security, global
See: *New World Order*

self-appointed
Antonym: *civic-minded*

self-confidence
Always desirable, no matter how unwarranted. Commonly presented as a vital sign of national political health.

USAGE: When you call for a new era of self-confidence, you will have the most impact when you appear to be doing so self-confidently. You may want to practice in front of a mirror. You certainly would be well advised to study video- and audiotapes, perhaps at variable speeds, with the guidance of trained professionals. You can best gain backers and influence voters if you exude what you are extolling—"self-confidence"—which, of course, is largely absent in society due to consequences of the flawed and failed approaches of politicians you oppose.

"I hope that the number one consequence of our victory in the Persian Gulf is that at long last we will have the national *self-confidence* to face up to our real problems here at home." (Arkansas governor Bill Clinton, May 6, 1991)
    Antonym: *self-doubt*
    See also: *crisis of confidence*

self-defeating patterns of behavior
An adroit phrase for pinning blame on victims of discrimination and unequal opportunities.

"It's time to shift the primary focus from racism, the

traditional enemy from without, to *self-defeating patterns of behavior,* the new enemy within." (Charles S. Robb, April 12, 1986)

See also: *behavior; pathology, tangle of*

self-determination

A goal for various people around the world, praised far more often than advanced by U.S. politicians. In rhetorical practice, usually a president's determination to be self-satisfied about how another country is being governed.

"We fight for the principle of *self-determination,* that the people of South Vietnam should be able to choose their own course. . . ." (Lyndon B. Johnson, January 12, 1966)

See also: *autonomy*

self-doubt

Always a bad sign, no matter how warranted.

USAGE: "Self-doubt" amounts to an excess of introspection, which you must always keep under tight control in public, since apparent certainty and evident self-satisfaction are far more lionized as emblems of leadership.

"We've come a long way since the decade of the seventies, years when the United States seemed filled with *self-doubt* and neglected its defenses, while the Soviet Union increased its military might and sought to expand its influence by armed forces and threat." (Ronald Reagan, January 16, 1984)

"One vision sees an America sealed off from the future, an America that would henceforth lock its doors to hide from the forces of history. It is a vision based on pessimism, fear, and *self-doubt.*" (Representative William S. Broomfield, May 23, 1991)

[Compare to Latin American writer Eduardo Galeano's comment in 1986: "I do not have a bad opinion of doubt. I think doubt has been a factor in the movement of history. I have grown to appreciate doubt more and more and, at the same time, to distrust those *compañeros* who only offer certainty. They seem too much like the wooden men which the Popol Vuh in Mayan mythology describes as one of the mistakes the gods made when they attempted to create man and didn't know how to construct him and finally they made him out of corn and he came out alright. But one of those attempts consisted of creating him out of wood. . . . We need neither fear doubt nor discouragement: they are the proof that our endeavors are human. And we are fortunate that these endeavors are human. Otherwise, these would be the endeavors of false men, men of wood, that is to say bureaucrats, dogmatic men, people who choose models over reality. Discouragement and doubt indicate that one sees reality as it really is."]

Antonym: *self-confidence*

See also: *crisis of confidence*

self-reliance

Often praised by politicians trying to put a damper on hopes for government assistance.

"Individual *self-reliance* and independence of spirit are the greatest sources of strength in this democracy of ours. They mark the difference between free countries and dictatorships." (Harry S Truman, December 5, 1950, speaking to the Midcentury White House Conference on Children and Youth.)

"Liberals have failed to emphasize hard work, *self-reliance,* and individual responsibility." (Senator Bill Bradley, July 19, 1991)

Modern derivation: Moynihan Report, written by Daniel Patrick Moynihan and released on August 9, 1965. The report urged that governmental agencies encourage black families to engage in "self-reliance" instead of expecting governmental actions to provide jobs and improve ghetto conditions.

self-righteous
Differently righteous.
USAGE: When accusing others of being "self-righteous," it may be possible to do so self-righteously even while coming across as an opponent of self-righteousness. Thus you have the potential of generating some emotional benefits of self-righteousness even while seeming to oppose it.

"It is becoming increasingly popular and politically safe for *self-righteous* Members to come to the Senate floor and deliver endless diatribes about the evils of tobacco and smoking." (Senator Jesse Helms, June 5, 1991)

self-styled
A sneering reference to what certain people choose to call themselves.

"It is nice to get out of Washington to see real people in hometown America. There are some folks who keep asking why I have to travel. The fact is that the President Bush Administration really does love to spend time with folks who make up the heart and soul of this nation, to see you, to discuss issues with you. Frankly, we'd rather listen to you than the *self-styled* experts in Washington." (White House chief of staff John H. Sununu, June 18, 1991)

See also: *self-appointed*

separation of powers
See: *balance of powers*

sheikdom
USAGE: Scornful word, helpful when you want to deride a particular Arab monarchy.

Antonyms: *moderate; our allies; responsible*

shore up
Bail out.
USAGE: Sounds better than "bail out."

"The odds are strong that the taxpayers are going to end up having to pay money to *shore up* the insurance fund" for the banking industry. (Representative Charles Schumer, June 11, 1991)

sick and tired of
USAGE: Sounds comfortably populist. Since a lot of people are sick and tired of a lot of things, you're bound to ring some bells, if only by rhetorical ricochet.

"We will continue our fight to establish waste watchdogs at each of the federal agencies. The American people are *sick and tired of* government scandals." (Representative Fred Upton, June 19, 1991)

significant impact
A benign-sounding euphemism for effects ranging up to the deaths of hundreds of thousands of people.

"There shouldn't be any doubt in anybody's mind that modern warfare is destructive, that we had a *significant impact* on Iraqi society that we wished we had not had to do." (Secretary of Defense Dick Cheney, June 22, 1991)

simplistic
Other politicians' competing solutions.

simplistic slogans
In contrast to one's own in-depth slogans.

sixties, the
Often the antihalcyon days representing supposed depravities.

"The U.S. is going back to a situation where we are confident with our position of leadership in world affairs. *The sixties* are over." (Representative Duncan Hunter, February 28, 1991)

See also: *Vietnam syndrome*

sixties retreads
Derisive term usually mouthed by those who never grasped the positive values that flowered during the 1960s.

"These tenured radicals, often *1960s retreads* . . ." (Syndicated columnist, TV network commentator, and behind-the-scenes Reagan debate coach George Will, May 6, 1991)

Synonyms: sixties radicals; *tenured radicals*

sleaze
USAGE: When it's your buddies, call it savvy, or don't talk about it. If it's the other side, call it "sleaze."

"The *sleaze* factor is slipping back into the White House." (Representative George Miller, June 8, 1991)

sleazeball
Kind of like a political spitball that struck out the home team.

"I think Roger Ailes ought to be an issue in this campaign. If that's the guy who's going to handle the president's communications strategy, then we ought to say so. If there's a *sleazeball* in American politics today, it's Ailes." (Michael Dukakis, June 22, 1991)

sleepless nights
USAGE: To explicate your sincerity, talk about your "sleepless nights" as you agonized over difficult political decisions. No one will criticize you for insomnia, so you can't lose.

See also: *anguish*

sloganeering
See: *simplistic slogans*

small business
USAGE: Don't forget to bow from time to time in the direction of this shrinking economic icon.

"The *small businesses* of America are the foundation of our cherished system of free, competitive enterprise." (Lyndon B. Johnson, May 24, 1966)

"We believe that America is a country where *small business* owners must succeed, because they are the bedrock, backbone of our economy." (Texas State treasurer Ann W. Richards, July 18, 1988)

"While the phrase has become cliché, the fact remains that *small business* is the backbone of this Nation." (Representative Jan Meyers, May 8, 1991)

"*Small business* is key to the success of our free enterprise system." (Representative Richard Baker, May 8, 1991)

"I am pleased to join my colleagues today to salute the real driving force of the American economy—*small businesses.*" (Representative Glenn Poshard, May 8, 1991)

"I don't want to be part of a party that wants to soak

small business people and working class people with an exorbitant Social Security tax while we cut capital gains for the wealthiest of our people." (Arkansas governor Bill Clinton, May 18, 1991)

smart bombs
Warheads with mechanical intelligence that may be inversely proportional to the wisdom of the person who ordered them fired; smart bombs, dumb president.

smear
An incoming accusation of variable accuracy that threatens to draw political blood.
   "The best and only answer to a *smear* or to an honest misunderstanding of the facts is to tell the truth." (Richard M. Nixon, September 23, 1952)

smoke and mirrors
The opposing side's contrived appearances.

smoke-filled rooms
USAGE: A dated expression—some key meetings of politicos even have "No Smoking" signs posted these days—but nowadays you might get even more mileage if you accuse opponents of frequenting "smoke-filled rooms."
   See also: *back room*

smoking gun
Ironclad certainty. A scandal's conclusion akin to the climax of a *Perry Mason* drama.
USAGE: If you want to undercut charges that have evident substance, keep insisting that the matter turns on whether there is a "smoking gun." This can help to raise the public perceptual threshold of proof so high that hopefully even

when weighty evidence has piled up, it will seem insufficient and inconclusive.

"If that memo had reached the hands of the President and he had approved it, that would be the *smoking gun.* . . . If that occurred—and let us emphasize the 'if'—that if it occurred, you would have a demand for impeachment proceedings." (Representative Lee Hamilton, June 14, 1987)

Antonym: *rumor and insinuation*

snooping
Antonym: *surveillance, lawful*

so help me God
An expression of pious humility in the midst of speechmaking.

"Your dreams, your hopes, your goals are going to be the dreams, the hopes, and the goals of this administration, *so help me God.*" (Ronald Reagan, January 20, 1981)

See also: *God's help*

soak-the-rich schemes
Scenarios for tax structures and other measures that would siphon some wealth away from the rich and distribute it for the benefit of others. Naturally, the rich and their flunky politicians denounce any such proposals, preferring the de facto continuation of soak-the-not-rich schemes.

social agenda
An agenda that does not fit with the speaker's.

USAGE: You can score points by emphasizing that—in contrast to your scrupulous impartiality—some people have ulterior motives for expressing themselves.

"I'm all for diversity, but I have a responsibility to intervene when they get into a *social agenda*." (Secretary of Education Lamar Alexander, June 26, 1991)

See also: *political agenda*

socialized

Of course, past proposals to establish such programs as Social Security, unemployment insurance, Medicare, and Medicaid were commonly denounced as attempts to impose a "socialized" system. But this red herring remains on many a politician's plate.

"The Democrats would love to see a *socialized* structure in health care, and no agenda on health care is going to satisfy their commitment to *socializing* health care until it meets that goal." (White House chief of staff John H. Sununu, June 16, 1991)

soldier-patriot

A favorable gloss for a military dictator.

"A *soldier-patriot* like Franco, General Pinochet saved his country from an elected Marxist who was steering Chile into Castroism." (syndicated columnist and former presidential speechwriter Patrick Buchanan, September 17, 1989)

Antonym: *military dictator*

soul of our country, soul of our nation

A person may or may not have a "soul," depending on the truth of various theologies. But a nation is unlikely to have one "soul."

"As we move toward 1992, the stakes are greater than the White House, for we are struggling for the *soul of our nation*." (Jesse Jackson, June 7, 1991)

". . . there is no room for these if the inner heart and

soul of our nation is to flourish." (Senator Jesse Helms, January 12, 1991)

"The fact is that the President Bush Adminstration really does love to spend time with folks who make up the heart and *soul of this nation,* to see you, to discuss issues with you." (White House chief of staff John H. Sununu, June 18, 1991)

"And when that first cocaine was smuggled in on a ship, it may as well have been a deadly bacteria, so much has it hurt the body, the *soul of our country.*" (George Bush, January 20, 1989)

"The true defense *of a nation* must be found in its own *soul. . . .*" (Dwight D. Eisenhower, February 1, 1951)

sound-bite
Brief broadcast snippets of an interview or speech.
USAGE: Disdain publicly, seek privately.

"There is a politics beyond the ten-second television *sound-bite.* Or at least there should be." (Senator Dan Coats, 1990)

special-interest contributors
People who give money to the opposition.

"They can't see beyond the end of their political strategists' noses as they confer with their six-figure *special-interest contributors* in fox-and-hound country. No wonder they can't communicate with working men and women anymore." (Republican National Committee chair Clayton K. Yeutter, June 21, 1991)

Antonym: civic-minded contributors to our campaign

special-interest groups
Organizations or constituencies supporting another candidate.

USAGE: The other side is in league with "special-interest groups"; you have no such backers, only public-spirited supporters who want what's best for all Americans.

"The provisions will not only save billions of dollars, but it will give us the opportunity to see who is serious about waste and who is not. To see who has more allegiance to *special-interest groups* than to the taxpayers who are paying the bills." (Senator Phil Gramm, February 1985)

"My campaign is kind of the opposite of Walter Mondale's in that regard. He had a bundle of programs for every *special-interest group;* now I have an array of things that will create more opportunity for everybody." (Pierre S. du Pont IV, January 16, 1988)

special interests

Formerly a term for well-financed forces trying to manipulate political decision-making with their large quantities of dollars, this pejorative is now usually aimed elsewhere—mostly at people who have more numbers and grievances than money or political power (such as feminists, racial minorities, the elderly, labor union members, and lesbian and gay rights backers).

USAGE: If you don't like them and you're not aligned with them, "special interests" is as good a put-down as any.

"It is easy to be misled by a small group of *special interests* engaged in a campaign of misrepresentation. We must not let the selfish demands of special groups blind us to the common good." (Harry S Truman, February 24, 1949)

"You know, national Democrats used to fight for the working families of America, and now all they seem to fight for are the *special interests.* . . . ." (Ronald Reagan, October 26, 1984)

"The existing immigration law works for the good of all the American people; it must not be treated like a *special interest* football to be kicked around at the whim of any militant group and its apologists in government." (Senator Jesse Helms, January 14, 1991)

"Our nation can no longer afford all of the wants of the many *special interests* we have in America." (Representative Wayne Allard, May 1991)

"Until most Members of Congress decide to vote for consumers and taxpayers, and against *special interests,* you can expect to pay more at the grocery store and to Uncle Sam." (Representative Harris W. Fawell, July 5, 1991)

Antonym: *constituents*

See also: *pressure group*

special relationship
A snappy phrase that extends to all manner of dubious or nefarious joint governmental ventures between the United States and allied nations, especially Great Britain and Israel.

"Establishing and maintaining friendly relations with the Arab states need not require the U.S. to tilt away from Israel or abandon the *special relationship* it now has . . . with Israel which must be preserved." (Jesse Jackson, 1988, campaign position paper)

special treatment
USAGE: What special interests are after, naturally.

"The truth is, despite the early clamor from individual interests demanding exemption and *special treatment,* there is no need for such punishing new taxes." (New York governor Mario M. Cuomo, February 13, 1991)

spend and spend and spend
Frugal rhetoric, cubed.

"Are you entitled to the fruits of your own labor or does

government have some presumptive right to *spend and spend and spend*?" (Ronald Reagan, July 27, 1981)

spendthrifts
See: *runaway spending*

spiraling cost of medical health care
Widely resented, and necessarily acknowledged by most politicians, who rarely challenge the corporations raking in huge profits from exorbitant medical bills.

"There are so many issues facing us as a country today and none is more important than resolving the *spiraling cost of medical health care* for everyone, including our senior citizens. For the most part, our enormous health care costs, which per capita are the highest in the world, are a result of our own economic and medical success. . . ." (Representative Alex McMillan, January 10, 1990)

Spirit of '76
See: *Founding Fathers; Valley Forge*

spiritual revival, hungering for a
Politicians as God-sent maitre d's.

"I have always believed that this country—not always, but in recent years, I should say, believed that this country is *hungering for a spiritual revival.*" (Ronald Reagan, February 9, 1982)

stability
Commonly, a situation in the world—no matter how unstable—that the U.S. government likes.

"There is some disagreement with our overall course in Vietnam. But even accepting our basic policy, it appears to me neither prudent nor wise to undertake risks of a still wider war until some progress has been made toward achieving the *stability* that is essential for the successful prosecution of our efforts in Vietnam." (Robert F. Kennedy, April 27, 1966)

"President Bush is to be commended. He . . . has demonstrated that we are willing and able to protect the security and *stability* of the Persian Gulf." (Senator Jesse Helms, January 12, 1991)

"Our purpose in the Persian Gulf remains constant: to drive Iraq out of Kuwait, to restore Kuwait's legitimate government, and to ensure the *stability* and security of this critical region." (George Bush, January 29, 1991)

See also: *balance of power; instability; moderate; our allies*

stand up

USAGE: People seem to like this one. After all, who can be against standing up? Implies courage; best used amid vague language to avoid the risk that favorable impressions might be disrupted by meaning.

"I want the Senators to *stand up* and to answer whether they are for the Communist Party, or against it." (Hubert Humphrey, 1954, introducing in the Senate a "Communist Control Act" aimed at virtually outlawing the Communist Party.)

"What this country needs, what the president needs, is a Congress that will *stand up* TO him in defense of the dollar at home and *stand up* WITH him in defense of freedom abroad." (Richard M. Nixon, March 6, 1966)

"There are so many times when there are issues or situations that are difficult and require you to really *stand up* against a lot of conflicting pressures, and I think having courage to *stand up* to do what is right for the country is probably the one thing you want in a president." (Representative Richard Gephardt, December 26, 1987)

stand up for America
USAGE: Why not?

"And I mean to try to serve my country with an unashamed patriotism. If enough of us do that—if enough of us *Stand Up for America*—we can stop America's retreat from victory. But the stakes are high. We know that if we fail, liberty in all the world might flicker and die for a thousand years." (George Wallace, 1972)

stay tuned
Keep watching and find out.
USAGE: A snappy answer to queries about plans on the policy drawing boards. Encourages journalists and the general public to view political events passively, as if watching a prerecorded TV show. Since this quiescent role is likely to resonate as comfortably familiar, many people may unconsciously feel a bit flattered when invited to "stay tuned" to find out what you will do.

"*Stay tuned.*" (George Bush, June 28, 1991, when asked about U.S. plans in relation to Iraq.)

stick
Ever since Theodore Roosevelt stressed the importance of brandishing a big one, politicians with an eye on the White House have tended to exalt the importance of having a sizable "stick."
USAGE: Apt to be invoked as a national endowment, to be swung by the president.

"[T]o confine our national posture to one of talking louder and louder while carrying a smaller and smaller *stick* —is to trade the long-range needs of the nation for the short-term appearance of security." (John F. Kennedy, June 14, 1960)

"And we must let the rest of the world know that we

speak softly, we carry a big *stick*, but we have the will and the determination, and if they ever hit us it is not going to stop us—we are just going to keep coming." (Lyndon B. Johnson, September 28, 1964)

"There was a great, great president a few years ago named Teddy Roosevelt who once said, 'Speak softly and carry a big *stick*.' Jimmy Carter wants to speak loudly and carry a fly swatter." (Gerald R. Ford, October 16, 1976)

"Big guy, six-four, tough. One time when I was less than truthful, he picked up a, I don't know whether it was a squash racket or a what, but it looked like a big *stick*. Remember Teddy Roosevelt, 'Speak softly and carry a big *stick*'? Well, my dad spoke LOUDLY and carried the same big *stick*. And he got our attention pretty quick! But he never really—he'd give us a lick once in a while, but he led by example. My dad was a leader, and everybody knew it." (George Bush, December 5, 1987)

Caution: Because confusing unconscious signals could result, may not be advisable for use by female candidates.

See also: *balls; kick ass; wimp*

stonewall
To deny real wrongdoing and to obstruct investigative efforts.
USAGE: You may need to accuse opponents of doing so at some junctures. But you should never publicly suggest that you or your aides could ever do such a thing. If you choose to pursue such a course of action in private, keep the discussion strictly in-house—and make damn sure there's no tape recorder running.

"I want you all to *stonewall* it." (Richard M. Nixon, March 22, 1973, transcribed from White House taping system.)

stooges
USAGE: If you really want to smear some reputations, refer to "stooges" while implying that they are puppets of hostile foreign powers or subversive ideologies. Be careful, however, to limit this epithet to individuals and groups lacking the money or prestige to be able to counterattack effectively.

See also: *unpatriotic*

strategic defense
New weapons systems under a defensive rubric.
USAGE: Whenever possible, refer to new weaponry you support as "strategic defense" technology.

"I think we should develop and deploy a *strategic defense,* and I think we should keep talking and negotiating." (Representative Jack Kemp, December 19, 1987)

See also: *modern weapons systems; national defense*

strategic importance
Value for geopolitical stratagems of Washington analysts and the multinational corporations whose profits they hold dear.

"But in Panama we face something more than human tragedy. We must confront complex issues of *strategic importance.*" (Senator Dan Coats, May 1989)

strategic interests, U.S.
See: *national interest*

streamline
USAGE: If you're trying to gut a government program, say your budget cuts will "streamline" its operations.

Antonym: *meat-ax approach*

street crime
See: *afraid to walk the streets; law and order*

strength
Commonly understood as military power—a preoccupation of presidents and would-be presidents, who seem unable or unwilling to recognize other kinds of strength.

"We will maintain sufficient *strength* to prevail if need be, knowing that if we do so we have the best chance of never having to use that *strength*." (Ronald Reagan, January 20, 1981)

"I had a plan when I came here first of all to be realistic about the . . . adversary relationship between the two nations, but also to deal from *strength*. That was why I was such a believer in refurbishing our military and our *strength*." (Ronald Reagan, November 28, 1987)

See also: *national security; weakness*

strength, a quiet
Military dominance, soft-spoken, perhaps with a smile.

"It is time for America to move and to speak not with boasting and belligerence but with *a quiet strength*. . . ." (Jimmy Carter, July 15, 1976)

"We are a strong nation, and we will maintain strength so sufficient that it need not be proven in combat—*a quiet strength* based not merely on the size of an arsenal, but on the nobility of ideas." (Jimmy Carter, January 20, 1977)

See also: *stick*

strident
A dismissive label for strongly expressed views that make politicians—and journalistic cohorts—uncomfortable.
USAGE: If antagonists turn up the heat, call them "strident."

"*Strident* emotionalism in the pursuit of truth, no matter

how disguised in the language of wisdom, is harmful to public policy, just as harmful as self-righteousness in the application of power." (Lyndon B. Johnson, May 11, 1966)

strongest, freest, wealthiest nation
A nationalistic mouthful.

"For more than 200 years, we've changed course when we've had to—overcoming the Articles of Confederation, foreign wars and civil war, recessions, depression, exclusion, division—to become the *strongest, freest, wealthiest nation* in the world. . . ." (New York governor Mario M. Cuomo, August 9, 1991)

superpower, only
"When we emerge from this war, we will be the *only superpower* on Earth." (Senator Phil Gramm, February 1991)

See also: *number one*

surgical strikes
A phrase that can make bombers dropping high-yield explosives on urban dwellers sound like scalpels in the hands of dedicated physicians fulfilling the Hippocratic oath.

See also: *tumor*

surveillance, lawful
Antonym: *snooping*

swift punishment for the guilty
See: *law and order*

system works, the
The moral of the story, between the lines of many a political tall tale.

take a stand
See: *stand up*

take it under advisement
USAGE: Nothing could be simpler. When you hear a suggestion that you have no interest in accepting, just say you'll "take it under advisement."
   See also: *advisory*

task force
See: *advisory*

tasteless joke
A dig that is not to the taste of the targeted politician.
USAGE: If a political rival tells a joke that rubs salt in a wound or is otherwise injurious to your image, you may want to fire back this way.
   "I heard that Senator Kohl last night made a totally *tasteless joke* about the time I spoke for four days in Atlanta, back in 1988. Those of you who were not there may not appreciate this, but believe it or not, I gave the speech I was asked to give at the length I was asked to give it." (Arkansas governor Bill Clinton, June 15, 1991)

tax and spend
Inevitable fiscal activities of a government, made to sound diabolical.
   "Beyond that, we must take further steps to permanently control government's power to *tax and spend.*" (Ronald Reagan, January 21, 1985)

tax burden
A heavy tone for references to taxation.
   "It is time to reawaken this industrial giant, to get gov-

ernment back within its means, and to lighten our punitive *tax burden*." (Ronald Reagan, January 20, 1981)

tax incentives
Tax breaks.

tax reform
A term so meaningless that in the 1980s, changes in federal taxation—shifts that cut tax rates for the rich and placed more burdens on others—were hailed as "tax reform."

"All my life I have heard promises about *tax reform,* but it never quite happens. With your help, we are finally going to make it happen. And you can depend on it." (Jimmy Carter, July 15, 1976)

See also: *reforms; regressive taxation*

taxes, no new
See: *revenue enhancement*

taxpayers
Always the much put-upon good guys.
USAGE: Remember, the taxpayers are always right. And you're always on their side.

"The American *taxpayers* are not going to stand for that, and neither am I." (Representative Henry B. Gonzalez, August 10, 1990)

taxpayers' expense, not printed at
USAGE: A typeset disclaimer to include whenever you put out a shred of paper without government funds. Of course, don't remind anyone when the government is footing the bill.

tears

USAGE: Your own tears should be visible or divulged only in contexts that are clearly religious, patriotic, and/or having to do with young people.

"And like a lot of people, I have worried a little bit about shedding *tears* in public, or the emotion of it. But as Barbara and I prayed at Camp David before the air war began, we were thinking about those young men and women overseas. And the *tears* started down the cheeks, and our minister smiled back, and I no longer worried how it looked to others." (George Bush, June 6, 1991)

See also: *under God*

technicality
See: *ambiguity; indiscretion*

technological edge
Often an edge for edge's sake, with a result of dubious or injurious high-tech.

"Finally, it should be noted that there are other serious economic consequences of the United States losing its *technological edge* in nuclear power." (former senator Paul E. Tsongas, March 1991)

Ten Commandments
USAGE: Generally quite a bit safer to defend than the Bill of Rights.

"Or as Labor Secretary Lynn Martin responded to a question about the need for more ethics laws, she said: 'All we really need is the *Ten Commandments*. The problem is that some people haven't read them yet.' I am constantly astounded by how many people fail to understand this." (Senator Warren B. Rudman, April 23, 1991)

tenured radicals

A term used to trash college professors who have unapproved opinions. For good measure, "tenured radicals" are accused of trying to suppress other views; these accusations often come from politicians and media commentators eager to suppress the views of the offending professors.

See also: *political correctness; radical; sixties retreads*

terrific

Much-abused superlative. Sometimes the rough translation is: "not terrible."

"It was a *terrific* speech. It was a little long because there were so many interruptions, but the delegates wanted to hear it." (Dukakis campaign chair Paul P. Brountas, July 20, 1988, describing convention speech by Arkansas governor Bill Clinton.)

See also: *dynamic; great*

terrorism

A label applied with careful and methodical selectivity. Thus—according to the vast majority of U.S. politicians and journalists—bombings, assassinations, and kidnappings are "terrorism" if done by Arabs, but not if done by Israelis.

"*Terrorism* is a growing threat, as evidenced by the increased targeting of innocent civilians engaged in innocent pursuits." (Ronald Reagan, February 6, 1986)

terrorists

Detested perpetrators of violent acts such as hostage-taking and murder—evil if denounced by the U.S. government.

Antonym: *commandos*

thermonuclear
USAGE: Avoid when referring to U.S. arsenal; sounds too ominous.

threat
Emanates only from adversaries, near and far.
USAGE: A "threat" can provide ever-expanding rationales. You get to define it as anything you choose so it can justify anything you want to do.

"If I conclude that increased enemy action jeopardizes our remaining forces in Vietnam, I shall not hesitate to take strong and effective measures to deal with that situation. This is not a *threat*. This is a statement of policy." (Richard M. Nixon, November 3, 1969)

"I would like to speak to you today of a rising *threat* to everything our servicemen have fought to accomplish in Southeast Asia—a *threat* embodied in the Hatfield-McGovern Amendment." (Spiro Agnew, August 17, 1970)

threat, Soviet
Obsolete.

threshold
Always the place where we're standing.

"As we meet here today, we stand on the *threshold* of a new era of peace in the world." (Richard M. Nixon, January 20, 1973)

"While we stand on the *threshold* of a great opportunity, the only thing we must remember is—the only thing that equals that opportunity is our obligation. . . ." (Democratic National Committee chair Paul G. Kirk, Jr., July 18, 1988)

See also: *crossroads of history*

throwbacks to the sixties
See: *sixties retreads*

thrust
Missile-launching power.
    See also: *stick*

tinhorn dictator
See: *two-bit dictator*

toilet seats, six-hundred-dollar
The lame liberal equivalent of a Reaganoid tale about a
welfare queen with a new Cadillac. As if the main problem
with Pentagon spending is that it's insufficiently frugal.
    See also: *lean and mean*

tolerance
Have you ever been tolerated?
    "And I've not the slightest doubt that this year once
again our national tradition of *tolerance* and fairness will
prevail." (Jimmy Carter, October 4, 1976)
    "The great challenge to all Americans—indeed to all free
men and women—is . . . above all else to keep in our
hearts and minds the *tolerance* and mutual trust that have
been the genius of American life throughout our history."
(Robert F. Kennedy, December 3, 1961)
    "Peace in our society involves more than economic
groups; it involves understanding and *tolerance* among all
creeds and races." (Dwight D. Eisenhower, September 19,
1956)
    "There is at least one defense against the atomic bomb.
That defense lies in our mastering this science of human
relationships all over the world. It is the defense of *toler-*

ance and of understanding, of intelligence and thoughtfulness." (Harry S Truman, May 11, 1946)

See also: *pluralism*

too many Indians

Part of an adage.

"Like Custer, who said there were *too many Indians,* I guess there were too many Democrats. I have this horrible problem in figuring this thing out. I can't think of anyone to blame except myself." (George Bush, November 1970, concession speech upon losing race for U.S. Senate in Texas.)

Caution: Not for use in areas where genocide of Native Americans is no longer looked upon favorably by most people.

See also: *manifest destiny*

torch has been passed

USAGE: Like many phrases identified with President Kennedy's inaugural address, this one has a lot of grand applications for newly elected officeholders.

"Let the word go forth from this time and place, to friend and foe alike, that the *torch has been passed* to a new generation of Americans—born in this century, tempered by war, disciplined by a hard and bitter peace, proud of our ancient heritage—and unwilling to witness or permit the slow undoing of those human rights to which this Nation has always been committed, and to which we are committed today at home and around the world." (John F. Kennedy, January 20, 1961)

See also: *new beginning; new spirit; renewal*

tough

Deserving of sympathetic admiration.

". . . but it is not, as we all know, an easy vote. We were

not elected to make the easy votes. We were elected to take on the *tough* ones as well." (Representative William S. Broomfield, January 12, 1991)

"[I decided to vote for the budget] because I had a responsibility. It was awfully *tough*. I wanted to make sure that when that budget is put on the governor's desk, that if there is not meaningful reform and cuts along with it he will veto it. I think I've done the right thing." (California Assembly member Paul V. Horcher, June 20, 1991)

tough choices
One's own decisions.

"This budget . . . makes *tough choices* in order to adhere to the requirements of the budget agreement." (House Budget Committee chair Leon E. Panetta, April 9, 1991)

See also: *hard choices*

tough legislation
USAGE: The only way to go when describing your remedy for crime and drugs.

"In Washington, I've been a supporter of *tough legislation* to deal with drug supply and law enforcement." (Senator Dan Coats, 1989)

tough problems
USAGE: You may as well make clear that you tackle them.

"Our way, the Democratic way, is to tackle the *tough problems.*" (Senator Lloyd M. Bentsen, July 21, 1988)

toughness
USAGE: Combine with an evocation of humane sensitivity for maximum synergistic effect—a kind of "tough love" in the political arena. Remember that to have something for

everyone at all times, you should be reassuring and pandering. Checks and balances are beneficial even for—and perhaps especially for—fervent rhetoric.

"The Dukakis-Bentsen ticket has the *toughness* to govern and the compassion to care about people." (Democratic National Committee chair Paul G. Kirk, Jr., July 18, 1988)

trade barriers
See: *protectionism*

trust, abuse the
USAGE: Can summon up imagery of a cruel adult who abuses a trusting child. Since this happens so much more often than you would ever want to address directly, this is a good way to tap in to some of the emotions of people with abuse in their childhood histories. You can at once reinforce the relationship of government to citizen as a paternalistic one, while insisting that the paternalism should be benevolent.

"We must never again *abuse the trust* of working men and women, by sending their earnings on a futile chase after the spiraling demands of a bloated Federal Establishment." (Ronald Reagan, January 21, 1985)

See also: *full picture*

truth, the
A purported absence of proven lies.
USAGE: Some philosophers tell us that truth is multifarious rather than singular. But as far as you need be concerned, facets of truth cannot severely contradict each other, and truth is best preceded by the article "the."

"Jimmy Carter . . . told *the truth*. He made this country strong." (former secretary of state Edmund S. Muskie, July 18, 1988)

"We believe that America deserves an administration that will obey the law, tell *the truth* and insist all who serve it do the same." (Senator Lloyd M. Bentsen, July 21, 1988)

"The most important thing is that this United States of America needs at least one political party that's not afraid to tell the people *the truth* and address the real needs of real human beings." (Arkansas governor Bill Clinton, May 6, 1991)

truth lies somewhere in between, the
Catchphrase indicating a meticulous effort to alienate few and reassure many as to one's commendable centrism.

"On the one side, advocates of nuclear power say the problem is meddling intervenors and regulatory bodies whose sole purpose in life is to stop nuclear power. On the other side, many antinuclear advocates see no redeeming features to nuclear power at all. I believe *the truth lies somewhere in between.*" (Representative John D. Dingell, February 26, 1991)

See also: *I do not mean to imply*

tumor
Uncle Sam stars as the world's preeminent surgeon. In this era of widespread cancer, people fear and abhor what "tumor" brings to mind. When depicting world trouble spots along those lines, even idiotic metaphors can sound convincing and comforting.

"There is a terrible sickness in the Middle East. We have tried every conceivable treatment, and nothing has worked. We must now lance the infected area and remove this *tumor.* Hussein has the option to render this *tumor* benign. It is his choice. But I think we all know that it is malignant and we must remove it before it is given a chance to spread. Mr. Speaker, to carry that analogy further, we must give the surgeons the tools to carry out their task. Short of the use of nuclear weapons, or chemical or biological weapons, we must give our fighting men and women every means they need to accomplish their task." (Representative Rod Chandler, January 11, 1991)

See also: *surgical strikes*

two-bit dictator

A dictator who deserves no quarter; merits more contempt than an upscale tyrant.

"We know that a sensible foreign policy does not invite a *two-bit dictator* to get rich selling drugs to our kids." (Senator John Kerry, July 19, 1988)

two choices

USAGE: To simplistify matters, explain that there are only "two choices" in a situation, one of which would have catastrophic results. Hopefully most people will be discouraged from imagining third or fourth possibilities.

"My fellow Americans, I am sure you can recognize from what I have said that we really only have *two choices* open to us if we want to end this war." (Richard M. Nixon, November 3, 1969)

tyrant, ambitious

Usually a despot who is too independent for his—and the U.S.A.'s—own good.

"Can anyone reasonably assert that it would serve our interests to mortgage the production and pricing levels of nearly one-half of the world's proven oil reserve to the whims of an *ambitious tyrant*? I think not." (Senator Warren B. Rudman, January 12, 1991)

See also: *ruthlessness*

Uu Vv

"U" is for Unite
"V" is for Voluntarism

---

ultimate capitalist
USAGE: Ultimate compliment.

"[Robert S.] Strauss is the *ultimate capitalist* if there ever was one. Just look at his client list, a page and a half of Fortune 500 companies." (Former Democratic Party chair John White, June 4, 1991)

ultimate price, the
Two meanings here for a quintessential politician. For public consumption, "the ultimate price" refers to loss of life while in the U.S. armed services. In private, it's more likely to be the dollar figure necessary for financial backers to swing a leveraged buyout, consummate an unfriendly takeover, or accumulate a campaign treasury sufficient for gaining higher office.
USAGE: Sounds grander and more transcendent than "death." Therefore, loved ones of American troops killed in action may feel a bit better to hear that their lost friends and relatives paid "the ultimate price" for a noble purpose. We must not leave a void in the air so that other, less properly patriotic attitudes might coagulate and be expressed in a socially disruptive manner.

"In particular, I want to express my sympathies to the families of those who have paid *the ultimate price* in the struggle for freedom. Their sacrifices will not be forgotten." (Representative Charles W. Stenholm, March 5, 1991)

ultraconservative
Too "conservative" for one's tastes.

ultraliberal
Too "liberal" for one's tastes.

unbeatable
Hubris, American-style.

"And the lesson from the Gulf War is that Americans—when properly motivated, led, and equipped—are *unbeatable*." (Representative Jolene Unsoeld, March 8, 1991)

See also: *number one; superpower, only*

Uncle Sam
National paternalism iconified. The strongest and kindest uncle anyone could ever want. Not to be confused with Uncle Donald.

"In short, while I would hope that we would continue to regard ourselves as members of the same family, I would also hope that *Uncle Sam*—like any political leader—would not neglect his family responsibilities in order to attend to his broader community responsibilities—or that he would confuse the two sets of issues. For inspiration and guidance as to what we can expect from our change in attitude and policies, we need look no further than right here in Puerto Rico." (John F. Kennedy, December 15, 1958)

under an air conditioner
USAGE: A deft way to conjure up images of federal officials as effete, remote, and possibly not very manly.

". . . it is one thing to sit in Washington in the Pentagon *under an air conditioner* and read about the plane and quite another to talk to the young people who are putting the plane through its paces." (Senator Phil Gramm, May 2, 1987)

See also: *fairies; Beltway, inside the*

under God

An expression of humility to guard against seeming overly proud or arrogant in national purpose.

"Mr. President, the times call for candor. The Philippines are ours forever. . . . We will not renounce our part in the mission of our race, trustee, *under God,* of the civilization of the world. . . . The Pacific is our ocean." (Senator Albert Beveridge, January 9, 1900)

"The unity of our country is a unity *under God.* It is a unity in freedom, for the service of God is perfect freedom." (Harry S Truman, February 3, 1951)

"As we are a nation *under God,* so I am sworn to uphold our laws with the help of God. And I have sought such guidance and searched my own conscience with special diligence to determine the right thing for me to do with respect to my predecessor in this place, Richard Nixon, and his loyal wife and family. . . . Now, therefore, I . . . do grant a full, free and absolute pardon unto Richard Nixon for all offenses against the United States. . . ." (Gerald R. Ford, September 8, 1974)

"We are a nation *under God,* and I believe God intended for us to be free." (Ronald Reagan, January 20, 1981)

"One people *under God* determined that our future shall be worthy of our past. . . . And may He continue to hold us close as we fill the world with our sound—sound in unity, affection, and love—one people *under God,* dedicated to the dream of freedom that He has placed in the human heart, called upon now to pass that dream on to a waiting and hopeful world." (Ronald Reagan, January 21, 1985)

"And I know that I believe deeply in a supreme being.

You see, this concept of one nation *under God* is more than rhetoric. It's something very very important to me, and I expect that some of that came from my mother and dad together, from a family—together—understanding that all of us needed a God in heaven." (George Bush, December 5, 1987)

". . . we really need to pause and ponder the strength that lies in each of our cities, for we are a nation *under God. . . .*" (House Speaker Jim Wright, July 18, 1988)

Antonym: *atheists*

undercut

What some members of Congress try to do to great presidents, according to presidential boosters—as if members of Congress have no right to go their own way.

USAGE: Naturally, if you're opposing the president's policy, then you're not trying to "undercut"—you're attempting to "restrain."

"Every major Democratic leader in both houses of Congress voted to *undercut* the president's position of leadership and to position themselves to the left of the United Nations." (Senator Phil Gramm, February 1991)

underdeveloped

An adjective for lands with massive poverty in comparison to other nations.

USAGE: Tinge such references with noblesse oblige and hardheadedness. Remember to place in a context conveying that you are neither a skinflint nor a sap when it comes to sharing American wealth with the poor nations.

"I think we have an obligation to help the *underdeveloped* countries. But I think we have to put a ceiling on foreign aid." (Gerald R. Ford, November 28, 1987)

Caution: Do not use this term for areas of the United

States where poverty is rampant. It is to be reserved for nations commonly seen as backward.

See also: *underprivileged*

underled
Overled, in the wrong directions.

"[The American people] are underorganized for the world economy, undereducated and *underled* and we should change it." (Arkansas governor Bill Clinton, June 15, 1991)

underprivileged
Euphemism for oppressed and ripped-off.

"While there is some controversy about 'school choice,' some of the reasoning behind it is to give to many of those *underprivileged* families that have no better alternatives for educating their children a chance to find a better school or at least having the leverage to force improvements in the schools their children now attend." (Representative George W. Gekas, June 21, 1991)

See also: *disadvantaged; less fortunate*

understands America
A high compliment about comprehension, as vague and ultimately unverifiable as it is subjective and presumptuous. USAGE: The complex totality of America may be unfathomable, but you are well advised to play along with pretenses of comprehending a national character, etc.

"And I couldn't be prouder both as a Texan and as a Democrat, because Lloyd Bentsen *understands America*— from the barrio to the board room. He knows how to bring us together. . . ." (Texas State treasurer Ann W. Richards, July 18, 1988)

See also: *caring*

unethical
See: *ethics*

uneven playing field
"Our companies are going forth to do one-on-one battle and are being mugged. Their competitors are aided by governments that aggressively seek out the advantages of *uneven playing fields* whenever possible." (former senator Paul E. Tsongas, March 1991)

Antonyms: *fair play; level playing field*
See also: *move the goalposts*

unfair preferences
"We will continue our vigorous enforcement of existing statutes, and I will once again press the Congress to strengthen the laws against employment discrimination without resorting to the use of *unfair preferences.*" (George Bush, January 29, 1991)

See also: *color-conscious; quotas*

unfair trade practices
Other countries' limitations and taxes on imports that work against U.S.-based corporations trying to sell products abroad.
USAGE: By definition, the United States does not engage in "unfair trade practices," so be careful never to imply that it does.

"My approach says, find the countries that have a pattern of *unfair trade practices* AGAINST the United States, and dispatch the President to negotiate with them to get rid of those practices for a two-year period. If they won't do it—are obstinate—then after a period of time give the President the power to begin penalizing their products coming here." (Representative Richard Gephardt, December 26, 1987)

uniform, men and women in
American troops, always heroic and inspirational, with confirmed seating on a nonstop through St. Peter's gates.

union bosses
A far more likely target for politicians' ire than management bosses—or political bosses.

"Recently, labor unions scored a victory as the U.S. House of Representatives voted them virtually limitless power through complete strike protection. If this union carte blanche isn't blocked, American business is certain to be held hostage to unyielding *union bosses.*" (Representative Bill Dickinson, July 30, 1991)

See also: *labor bosses, big*

unite
The ostensible purpose becomes almost secondary, since the call to "unite" is often intended to drown out or suppress dissenting voices.

"Every night before I turn out the lights to sleep I ask myself this question: 'Have I done everything that I can do to *unite* this country? Have I done everything I can to help *unite* the world, to try to bring peace and hope to all the peoples of the world? Have I done enough?' " (Lyndon B. Johnson, April 7, 1965)

"Put away all the childish divisive things, if you want the maturity and the *unity* that is the mortar of a nation's greatness." (Lyndon B. Johnson, May 17, 1966)

"As long as the Vietnamese foe feels that he can win something by propaganda in the country—that he can undermine the [U.S.] leadership—that he can bring down the government—that he can get something in the Capital that he can't get from our men out there—he is going to keep on trying. But I point out to you that the time has come when we ought to *unite*, when we ought to stand up and be counted." (Lyndon B. Johnson, March 18, 1968)

"For the more divided we are at home, the less likely the enemy is to negotiate in Paris. Let us be *united* for peace. Let us be *united* against defeat. Because let us understand: North Vietnam cannot defeat or humiliate the United States. Only Americans can do that." (Richard M. Nixon, 1969)

"The resolution we now bring before the House is a statement of national purpose. It is a vote of confidence in the President on our gulf policy and a confirmation that America is *united*." (Representative William S. Broomfield, January 12, 1991)

"Now is not the time for partisan politics. Now is the time for Republicans, Democrats, and people of all parties and philosophical persuasions to *unite* as Americans behind our President and send a clear message to Saddam Hussein that our resolve is firm and that we speak with one voice. Those democratic institutions that last the longest, Mr. President, jealously guard both diversity and dissent in society as a matter of eternal law. Yet to prosper, a free people must also *unify* in a crisis and know the time when a protracted debate can send a mixed signal to a dangerous adversary." (Senator John Seymour, January 12, 1991)

unpatriotic
A guided missile in bombastic arsenals.
    See also: *stooges*

unprovoked aggression
Accusational overkill; if it was provoked it probably wouldn't qualify as "aggression."

"When we went in, we went in because it was the right thing to do, and we went in because we did not think that *unprovoked aggression* should be permitted to succeed, and we went in because we had some substantial national interests at stake. You can't say you're doing this to keep the world safe for democracy, because these aren't democracies that you're going in here to assist. But it was still the right thing to do." (Secretary of State James A. Baker III, May 23, 1991, explaining why the United States went to war with Iraq.)

See also: *naked aggression*

untutored squirts
Insufficiently conditioned.

"I went in there [the CIA] when it had been demoralized by the attacks of a bunch of little *untutored squirts* from Capitol Hill, going out there, looking at these confidential documents without one simple iota of concern for the legitimate national security interests of this country." (George Bush, June 1987)

Valley Forge
It's been a long time since U.S. armed forces lived like the patriots at Valley Forge in the midst of the Revolutionary War—in fact, independence-minded guerrilla armies up against modern U.S. weaponry have often lived under such conditions in recent decades—but the U.S.A.'s post-1945 policies of counterinsurgency haven't staunched the bleeding rhetoric here at home.

USAGE: Helpful for cranking up stem-winders of a patriotic-religious nature. Allusions to inclement weather are almost mandatory.

"And unless this task is accomplished, as we move into the most critical period in our nation's history since that bleak winter at *Valley Forge,* our national security, our survival itself, will be in peril." (John F. Kennedy, June 14, 1960)

"It's been written that the most sublime figure in American history was George Washington on his knees in the snow at *Valley Forge.* He personified a people who knew that it was not enough to depend on their own courage and goodness, that they must also seek help from God—their Father and preserver." (Ronald Reagan, February 9, 1982)

"Now we hear again the echoes of our past: a general falls to his knees in the hard snow of *Valley Forge.* . . ." (Ronald Reagan, January 21, 1985)

"My friends, the dream that began in Philadelphia 200 years ago, the spirit that survived that terrible winter at *Valley Forge* and triumphed on the beaches at Normandy, the courage that looked Khrushchev in the eye during the Cuban missile crisis is as strong and as vibrant today as it has ever been." (Michael Dukakis, July 21, 1988)

See also: *Founding Fathers*

values, American
A quintessential national product, seemingly ideal for export.
USAGE: Speak as if "American values" are unique moral beliefs and achievements that the rest of the world will find awesome and well worth buying. You might add that the transaction has been thwarted by the relative backwardness of other societies and/or by a shortage of wisdom among some U.S. politicians.

". . . . most of these disputes in the Third World really

don't involve direct confrontations between the Soviet Union and America. What they really are is an opportunity to sell *American values.* I think Central America is a perfect example of that." (Bruce E. Babbitt, January 16, 1988)

"This Nation deserves a foreign policy based on the *values* that unite us as *Americans.* . . ." (Jimmy Carter, July 18, 1988)

". . . this election is . . . about *American values,* old-fashioned values, like accountability and responsibility and respect for the truth." (Michael Dukakis, July 21, 1988)

"Tonight, at the risk of being further charged with divisiveness, insensitivity and mediocrity, I want to continue my discussion of the deterioration of *American values* in many of our institutions of higher education." (Spiro Agnew, April 28, 1970)

See also: *values, Western*

values, Christian
Values consistent with the politician's definition of true Christianity.

See also: *anti-Christian*

values, ethical
USAGE: This is a no-lose combo. Very few people are against "ethical values."

"I know I believe in these *ethical values* and the stuff we're talking about here." (George Bush, December 5, 1987)

See also: *ethics; moral base; moral fiber*

values, family
The positive values instilled by families, but not the negative ones.

USAGE: Since the values that actually hold sway in families

vary a great deal, you'll probably want to use "family" as a hazy adjective denoting goodness.

"Rebuilding America begins with restoring family strength and preserving *family values.*" (Ronald Reagan, February 9, 1982)

"I speak really to the great mainstream of America on issues, whether it's *family values,* whether it's balanced budget, whether it's strong national defense." (Pat Robertson, February 13, 1988)

"Rest assured that I will continue to stand up for traditional *family values,* fiscal responsibility, and our system of free enterprise." (Representative Mel Hancock, December 1990)

See also: *American family, the; family; pro-family*

values, old
Like wines, assumed to be better when they are aged. Of course, such assumptions must bypass some of the most cruel and alienating "values" that have their roots in human antiquity.

"Our burden is to give the people a new choice rooted in *old values.*" (Arkansas governor Bill Clinton, May 6, 1991)

values, shared
USAGE: This phrase is wonderfully ambiguous and inclusive, a synergy of qualities that makes it ideal for many occasions.

"We come from different backgrounds, pursue different interests, and hold different views, but we can draw communion from our *shared values.*" (Ronald Reagan, February 9, 1982)

"And I'm eager to undertake with those on this platform what I hope will be a journey of *shared values,* a common pursuit of uncommonly important goals." (California governor Pete Wilson, January 7, 1991)

values, traditional

USAGE: Most effective when targeted voters feel threatened by changes in social mores and beliefs.

"If we have come to the point in America where any attempt to see *traditional values* reflected in public policy would leave one open to irresponsible charges, then I say the entire structure of our free society is threatened." (Ronald Reagan, February 9, 1982)

See also: *values, old*

values, Western

A reference to all the truly uplifting and inspiring aspects of Western societies, without alluding to the fact that those societies also brought the world such phenomena as far-flung colonialism, the atomic bomb, the Vietnam War, ozone depletion, global warming, and other glitches.

USAGE: A grand way to equate Western countries with the best moral orientations on the planet. It's also a slick way to imply something that would be impolitic to say straight out —that societies outside the West are relatively crude or depraved in their values.

"What's happened in Asia, I think, is a striking, a stunning, vindication of *Western values,* of market economics, of the yearning for freedom, and that in a sense what American policy must now be aimed at is taking yes for an answer." (Bruce E. Babbitt, January 16, 1988)

See also: *values, American*

vendetta, personal
USAGE: If you're on the political ropes and feeling very beat up, try complaining to anyone who'll listen that you are the victim of a "personal vendetta."

very simple, it's
Very simplistic.
   "Now if we want to stop AIDS, *it's very simple*. We should go back to sexual abstinence outside of marriage and fidelity within marriage." (Pat Robertson, February 13, 1988)

Vietnam syndrome
A diagnosis of public aversion to U.S. involvement in warfare because of the Vietnam War. Opponents and supporters of military interventions depict the significance of this "syndrome" to suit their current argument.
   See also: *Vietnams, no more*

Vietnams, no more
USAGE: A superb Rorschach phrase. Very few Americans have pleasant associations with the Vietnam War. By insisting that such an experience must not be repeated, you can garner support from constituencies that disagree strongly with each other. Hawks are likely to assume you wish that the U.S. military had been allowed to be even more destructive in Vietnam; doves may interpret the phrase as a commitment to prevent such massive slaughter in the future.
   "No more Vietnams!" (Representative Rod Chandler, January 11, 1991, just before voting to authorize the United States to wage war on Iraq.)

vigilance
The more eternal the better.

violence
The violence that is being opposed; not to be confused with
the violence that is official policy, such as warfare.

"The wanton destruction of property, gangsterism, arson,
and gunfire will only destroy the framework of justice and
law we are laboring to build. No responsible public official
can condone *violence* any more in Los Angeles than in Mississippi." (Hubert H. Humphrey, August 23, 1965)

"We cannot condone or excuse *violence*—whatever the
cause—nor can we overlook the role of hoodlums and agi-
tators in certain of the disorders." (Hubert H. Humphrey,
August 26, 1966)

"We will not endure *violence.* It matters not by whom it is
done or under what slogan or banner. It will not be tolerated. This Nation will do whatever it is necessary to do to
suppress and to punish those who engage in it." (Lyndon B.
Johnson, July 24, 1967, after authorizing use of federal
troops in Detroit.)

"The apostles of *violence,* with their ugly drumbeat of
hatred, must know that they are now heading for ruin and
disaster." (Lyndon B. Johnson, July 27, 1967)

vision
To be provided to the body politic by remarkably wise social
optometrists who have hung out their political shingles.
USAGE: A boilerplate response when called upon to name
the most important quality of a leader.

"The American people cannot afford to trust their future
to men of little *vision.*" (Harry S Truman, October 25, 1948)

"I am running for President because I have a *vision* of a
new America, a different America, a better America, and it

is not shared by those who are trying so hard to stop my campaign." (Jimmy Carter, May 27, 1976)

"We candidates ask the people for your votes. You, in turn, ask us for our *vision*." (Jimmy Carter, May 28, 1976)

"*Vision*—an understanding about the future, how to bring out the potential of a country and a people and each individual. . . . [T]here's one thing people will not forgive you—they will not forgive a lack of *vision*. They will not forgive you for not looking forward. And I think basically that is what American politics and political experience is all about." (Representative Jack Kemp, December 19, 1987)

"I think he has to have *vision*. A leader has to see beyond the minutiae of the moment and chart a course that will take the country into the next decade and maybe the next century." (Pat Robertson, February 13, 1988)

"Paul Kirk . . . has given us *vision*. He's given us strength. He's put us on the right course." (Democratic National Convention Rules Committee chair Kathleen M. Vick, July 18, 1988)

"While there are certain things that my staff and I have to do, we are really here to promote a *vision* and a mission." (Senator Phil Gramm, January 1990)

"The time has come for a New American Mandate, based on the precious values of the past but focused on a *vision* of the future." (former senator Paul E. Tsongas, March 1991)

vision, scorn our
See the world differently from how we want them to. Hell hath no fury like our vision scorned.

"There are those in the world who *scorn our vision* of human dignity and freedom." (Ronald Reagan, January 21, 1985)

vital interests

"We cannot ask for a reprieve from responsibility while freedom is in danger. The *vital interests* of the United States require us to stay in the battle. We dare not desert." (Lyndon B. Johnson, March 19, 1964)

See also: *national interest*

vocal minority

People who are too loud for their numbers, and presumably wrong to boot.

USAGE: A nice touch for suggesting that people making a lot of noise in favor of a certain position must be out of step.

"If a *vocal minority,* however fervent its cause, prevails over reason and the will of the majority, this nation has no future as a free society." (Richard M. Nixon, November 3, 1969)

Antonyms: *courageous voices; prophetic minority*

voluntarism, volunteerism

People doing good things that the government has refused to provide funds for.

"If I become President, I intend to strengthen the American system of private *volunteerism* that is imperative if this nation is to meet its commitment for basic social justice." (Jimmy Carter, October 4, 1976)

"I see national pride restored. I see a revival of patriotism. I see an outpouring of a sense of *volunteerism.*" (Jimmy Carter, October 27, 1976)

The Salvation Army is an "organization that epitomizes the *voluntarism* that is America." (Senator Phil Gramm, October 31, 1987)

See also: *neighbor caring for neighbor; points of light, a thousand*

voluntary guidelines
Toothless platitudes made to sound like substantial measures.
   Synonym: optional standards
   See also: *nonbinding*

voodoo
Ostensibly denoting an antithesis of empirical disciplines, this adjective gains part of its power by evoking jungle dwellers ignorant of the scientific method.
USAGE: Ever since George Bush castigated Ronald Reagan for "voodoo economics" during the 1980 presidential primary campaign, it's been routine for politicians to fling "voodoo" as a disparaging brickbat. The ethnocentric echoes are unrecognized enough that your risk of drawing flak on such grounds is small indeed.
   "Don't the Republicans get it? Trickle-down doesn't work. It's *voodoo* economics." (Representative Richard Gephardt, June 11, 1991)
   "It's time to rekindle the American spirit of invention and daring, to exchange *voodoo* economics for can-do economics, to build the best America by bringing out the best in every American." (Michael Dukakis, July 21, 1988)
   See also: *can-do*

Ww Xx

"W" is for War on Drugs
"X" is for Xenophobia

waiver
Antonym: loophole

war, the ugliness of
USAGE: The more you're inclined to favor military action, the more you should go out of your way to decry war in general terms.

"I think I'd be a better President because I was in combat. . . . I think I'd be a little more sensitive about sending somebody else's kid off to war because I saw that, *the ugliness of war*." (George Bush, December 5, 1987)

war criminals
Only warfare's victors, of course, can hope to convene war crimes trials. In any event, scenarios for prosecution tend to vary widely (e.g., most Americans would consider Saddam Hussein to be an obvious defendant, while surviving relatives of many thousands of Iraqi civilians killed by order of George Bush might have other thoughts).
USAGE: Here's a chance to uncork the oratory and let it flow with politically beneficial righteousness. The Lord, having said that "vengeance is mine," nevertheless can use some avenging angels now and again. Besides, you can fill press releases and newsletters to constituents with fiery statements about the need for prosecution of the foreign despots most reviled in the United States.

"Justice delayed is justice denied. I am also concerned that the longer this process drags on, the greater the possibility that public interest will wane and one of the most notorious *war criminals* in recorded history [Saddam Hussein] will get off scot-free." (Representative William S. Broomfield, May 21, 1991)

See also: *America means business*

war on crime
See: *law and order*

war on drugs
For righteous breast-beating, this one can't be beat.
USAGE: Let's face it, most Americans are fond of war metaphors. Since for most of them "war" has never been anything other than a metaphor or faraway spectacle, cranked-up war verbiage tends to excite them—at least intermittently, when substantial numbers of your colleagues find it appropriate to whip up some more hysteria. Of course, drugs will always be around, and many of the legal ones are addling the brains and destroying the livers and lungs of millions who nod in agreement or nod off when you're letting loose with another "war on drugs" salvo—but if you can't wink at hypocrisy while playing along with it, you really ought to find another line of work.

"We must aggressively push forward on the *war on drugs*. There must be no quarter given to traffickers, no place to hide from the force and the rule of the law." (Washington governor Booth Gardner, July 18, 1988)

See also: *drug problem; drugs*

war on poverty
Obsolete.
". . . I have called for a national *war on poverty*. Our

objective: total victory." (Lyndon B. Johnson, March 16, 1964)

"The *war on poverty* will be pressed forward until this bitter word 'poverty' is banished not only from our lives, but hopefully even from the language we speak." (Hubert H. Humphrey, April 2, 1966)

"The *war on poverty* is being administered to eradicate the stagnant pools of bitterness and frustration which breed much of our present-day crime." (Hubert H. Humphrey, May 25, 1966)

"The *war on poverty,* like it or not, is the single outstanding commitment this nation has made to the principle that poverty must be abolished." (Robert F. Kennedy, October 3, 1966)

See also: *Great Society*

Washington insiders
See: *Beltway, inside the; insiders*

waste
USAGE: To fail to fulminate against it at frequent intervals would be a real waste. Not to be confused with nuclear waste, which you tacitly support by virtue of backing nuclear weapons production, if not atomic power plants.

"The provisions will not only save billions of dollars, but it will give us the opportunity to see who is serious about *waste* and who is not." (Senator Phil Gramm, February 1985)

"I believe that *waste* is a crime. I believe that *waste* is against our freedom. I believe that *waste* is against our progress. Thus, I believe that *waste* is against the American people." (Lyndon B. Johnson, April 5, 1966)

waste-free government spending
USAGE: Although some waste is inevitable, claiming it could be eliminated may sound earnest and idealistic. Though perhaps dull, this refrain can keep you aligned with the forces of frugal goodness against the forces of bureaucratic evil. That way you're guaranteed to stay on the losing but holy side.

"This bill goes a long way towards my goal of *waste-free government spending*. Specific program goals, with clearly stated objectives, will force regular evaluations of government programs to earmark the cost-efficient and weed out the wasteful." (Representative Bill Archer, April 17, 1991)

wasteful spending
Always good for ritual denunciation.

"Our war against *wasteful spending* is far from over. Those members of Congress who voted to increase spending for Congressional mail are accountable to their constituents and their constituents should demand to know why they voted the way they did." (Representative Fred Upton, June 5, 1991)

way of life
Diverse and changing; usually alluded to as if singular and static.

"The defense of freedom, I believe, is a duty which falls to every individual who cherishes our *way of life*." (Senator Daniel K. Inouye, January 12, 1991)

See also: *American way, the*

we Americans
Some Americans.

"These are not appropriate subjects for narrow partisan oratory. They go to the heart of what *we Americans* are all about—all of us, Democrats and Republicans." (Lyndon B. Johnson, January 17, 1968)

"Although government has its limits and cannot solve all our problems, *we Americans* reject the view that we must be reconciled to failures and mediocrity, or to an inferior quality of life." (Jimmy Carter, July 15, 1976)

"*We Americans* have little tolerance for tyrants. We have even less when they threaten our national interests." (Senator Dan Coats, May 1989)

See also: *all Americans; American people, the; people, the*

we do not seek its overthrow

We seek its overthrow.

"But let us be clear as to the American attitude toward the government of Nicaragua. *We do not seek its overthrow.*" (Ronald Reagan, April 27, 1983)

weakness

Eschewed as a temptation for overseas foes—a timeworn rationale for building up the U.S. military even more.

"We dare not tempt them with *weakness.* For only when our arms are sufficient beyond doubt can we be certain beyond doubt that they will never be employed." (John F. Kennedy, January 20, 1961)

"But to all those who would be tempted by *weakness,* let us leave no doubt that we will be as strong as we need to be for as long as we need to be." (Richard M. Nixon, January 20, 1969)

"We are a purely idealistic Nation, but let no one confuse our idealism with *weakness.*" (Jimmy Carter, January 20, 1977)

wedge issue
Political pro shop talk for what *Newsweek* (May 27, 1991) defined as "a rhetorical opportunity to rile up the voters."

welcome them to American technology
Kill them.

"When the Iraqis come out of their bunkers, whatever they come out of, your A-6 Intruder is going to *welcome them to American technology.*" (Senator Phil Gramm, February 11, 1991)

welfare
An array of government assistance programs for the indigent.
USAGE: Since many people approve of programs lumped together as "welfare" but don't like the name, the more you support funding "welfare" the less you should refer to it that way, and vice versa. For an extra snappy presentation to justify cutbacks in spending for such programs, make it a point to contrast "welfare" with "work," so you can appeal to self-righteousness among those who have a job. And if you're pushing to cut funds for kids, go out of your way to stress that you care about children and that you want to reduce expenditures for their own long-term good.

"Let us remember that America was built not by government, but by people—not by *welfare,* but by work—not by shirking responsibility, but by seeking responsibility." (Richard M. Nixon, January 20, 1973)

"We've lost the spirit in our nation. A spirit of youth, vigor, a spirit of confidence, self-reliance, a spirit of work and not of *welfare,* a spirit of . . ." (Jimmy Carter, September 27, 1976)

"In the *welfare* culture, the breakdown of the family, the

most basic support system, has reached crisis proportions. . . ." (Ronald Reagan, February 6, 1986)

"But treating *welfare* as a socially acceptable permanent
lifestyle is a disservice to AFDC children. . . . Wholly
apart from the government's financial straits, we must
never—if we care about poor children—permit *welfare* to
be accepted as anything but a transition from dependency
to independence and the dignity that goes with it." (California governor Pete Wilson, January 10, 1991, announcing a
state budget plan that would reduce payments for the Aid
to Families with Dependent Children program.)

See also: *benign neglect; big government; paternalism*

welfare cheats/chiselers/fraud
USAGE: If few of your constituents are poor.

welfare state
See: *socialized*

we're all very proud of
USAGE: When you are trumpeting a majority viewpoint that
nevertheless has some detractors, this phrase is useful for
rendering all dissenters invisible, as if they don't really exist
or certainly don't matter.

"My message today is that while *we're all very proud of*
our military victory in the Persian Gulf, we all know that all
is not well in America." (Arkansas governor Bill Clinton,
May 18, 1991)

See also: *all Americans*

Western civilization
USAGE: Broad and safe. Note, however, that you will have
no occasion to speak in similar terms of "Eastern civilization."

"I believe in *Western civilization* and its moral power. I believe deeply in the principles the West esteems." (Ronald Reagan, June 9, 1982)

See also: *values, Western*

wheel of destiny

A kind of rigged *Wheel of Fortune,* with the president as Pat Sajak and the first lady as Vanna White.

"Today we have become the strongest and richest nation in the world, and the *wheel of destiny* has turned so that any hope the world has for the survival of peace and freedom will be determined by whether the American people have the moral stamina and the courage to meet the challenge of free-world leadership." (Richard M. Nixon, November 3, 1969)

See also: *destiny; moral stamina*

wheeler-dealers

See: *back room; smoke-filled rooms*

white hats

Private verbal shorthand for allies.

wimp

An epithet so injurious in the macho electoral arena that its sting can be felt for many years.

"You're talking to the *wimp.* You're talking to the guy that had a cover of a national magazine, that I'll never forgive, put that label on me." (George Bush, June 16, 1991) Bush was referring to a 1988 *Newsweek* cover. But he provided an exclusive article to *Newsweek*—titled "Why We Are in the Gulf" and published under his byline in the magazine's November 26, 1990 issue—about the evils of

Iraq's Saddam Hussein. The exigencies of propaganda can require that such grudges be suspended.

win decisively

To many a politician's mind, the only way to resolve a war that the United States is fighting.

"[The U.S. policy in Vietnam] was bad because if we decided to shed one drop of American blood, it should be under a formula in which we had intended to take all of the actions necessary to win—and *win decisively* and promptly." (Alexander M. Haig, January 30, 1988)

See also: *Vietnams, no more*

win the peace

Dominate after the war.

"You have often heard it said, I think that public opinion wins wars. And I would say with respect to that, in adapting it to the terms of peace, that only an informed public opinion can *win the peace*." (Dwight D. Eisenhower, April 24, 1950)

"I pledged in my campaign for the Presidency to end the war in a way that we could *win the peace*. I have initiated a plan of action which will enable me to keep that pledge. The more support I can have from the American people, the sooner that pledge can be redeemed." (Richard M. Nixon, November 3, 1969)

"American leadership has won the war and will now *win the peace*." (Representative Charles W. Stenholm, March 5, 1991)

Antonym: *lose the peace*

window of opportunity
An opening for strategic advantage.
USAGE: You'll want to warn that it will slam shut, unutilized, if your program is not implemented.

work
Except for fighting wars, perhaps the most lionized activity in the American political lexicon, no matter how low-paid, monotonous, demeaning, enervating, or dead-end the exalted labor may be.

"We should invest more in people on welfare, to give them the skills they need to succeed and to help them with child care and with medical care for their children, but we should demand that everybody who can go to *work* do it. For *work* is the best social program this country has ever devised." (Arkansas governor Bill Clinton, May 6, 1991)

"How are you going to get ahead in the world? By hard *work*—that was always the American way. But now, no longer do our people take pride in good *work* well done." (Dwight D. Eisenhower, November 1966)

work ethic
Often the touted belief that others should work as hard, give work as high a priority—and define "work" in the same terms—as one assumes is appropriate for their circumstances.

"These forebearers created a nation with an enduring *work ethic,* a sense of personal discipline, and an acute appreciation of the common good. They had a sense of purpose. . . ." (former senator Paul E. Tsongas, March 1991)

"The welfare policies of the past twenty-five years have encouraged a debilitating dependency and discouraged the *work ethic* that has made America strong." (Representative Harris W. Fawell, July 15, 1991)

work, plenty of
USAGE: Implying that the unemployed ignore available jobs can encourage people with jobs to doubt the integrity of those who haven't found employment.

"There is *plenty of work* to do if people would do it." (Henry Ford, March 1931)

working class
USAGE: Acceptable for occasional use. However, you must never publicly speak of a "ruling class" in a domestic context.

"*Working class* families put in more hours at work and less time with their children in 1989 than they did in 1979." (Arkansas governor Bill Clinton, May 6, 1991)

". . . a new voice was heard—the voice of an unknown preacher serving a *working class* community in Detroit. Ever since that time, Reinhold Niebuhr has been taming cynics and pulling utopians back to earth." (Hubert H. Humphrey, February 25, 1966)

working families
Implicitly more laudable and deserving than unemployed families.
USAGE: A good phrase for implying to people with jobs that you consider them to be of higher priority than the jobless. Such phrasing can subtly appeal to the employed majority of voters while hopefully not alienating the unemployed.

"During my entire lifetime, from farm boy to nominee of the Democratic Party for President of the United States, I've always been close to the *working families* of this nation." (Jimmy Carter, September 6, 1976)

". . . Franklin Roosevelt, and Harry Truman, and John Fitzgerald Kennedy, and Hubert Humphrey, and Scoop Jackson. Every one a Democrat—unafraid of change and confident of the future. Every one a friend of the *working families* of America, and every one a public model of confidence and fairness. . . . Along the march to victory, this party stopped to listen to the voices of *working families* all across this country." (Democratic National Committee chair Paul G. Kirk, Jr., July 18, 1988)

"This budget is aimed directly at the needs of America's *working families*." (House Budget Committee chair Leon E. Panetta, April 8, 1991)

See also: *welfare*

world's policeman, the
USAGE: Naturally you don't want the United States to be "the world's policeman." That said, you are unencumbered if you want to explain just how the U.S. government should police the world in any specific instance.

wrangling, partisan
See: *partisan; partisan bickering*

xenophobia
Other people's hostility toward foreigners. Not our own.
See also: *nationalistic*

Yy Zz

"Y" is for Youth
"Z" is for Zealous

young people
The objects of interminable praise from political podiums, even more laudable since the voting age dropped from twenty-one to eighteen.

"I have been fortunate that my own life has been spent with America's *young people*. . . . My faith in them is my unbounded faith in America itself." (Dwight D. Eisenhower, June 10, 1953)

"America's greatest asset will always be our *young people*." (Lyndon B. Johnson, June 30, 1965)

"To the *young people* of our country—and I'm so happy to see so many of them here—let me, if I could, say to you *young people:* You are what this election is all about—you and your future. Your generation is something special. Your love of country and idealism are unsurpassed. . . . I've seen you all across this country, and you are special. . . ." (Ronald Reagan, October 26, 1984)

youth
USAGE: Always the nation's shining promise of the future, etc.

"We see the hope of tomorrow in the *youth* of today. I know America's *youth*. I believe in them." (Richard M. Nixon, January 20, 1969)

youthful indiscretion
USAGE: If old skeletons start rattling loudly, you might try this phrase for damage control.

zealots
Extremely enthusiastic and energized persons in an opposing camp.
   See also: *fanatics*

zealous
Too committed and outspoken.
   "As long as the cameras roll and the newspapers carry the story, tobacco will continue to be a whipping boy for *zealous* antismokers." (Senator Jesse Helms, June 5, 1991)
   Antonym: dedicated

Acknowledgments

When *The Power of Babble* was a mere gleam in my eyes, Daniel Levy got behind it. An astute and creative editor at Dell, he remained supportive every step of the way.

Laura Gross, a wonderful literary agent, encouraged and sustained this book from the outset.

Special research help came from Ross Dendy, Kim Deterline, Steve Rhodes, and Miriam Solomon. Under tight deadlines, Chris Shein and Jamilah Vittor searched libraries and found many rhetorical treasures. Melissa Bernstein and John Cowan pitched in at a crucial time. Paul Blue, Max Greenberg, and Grant Wilson backed the research. And Bob DeBolt kept providing an array of valuable resources.

At the media watch group FAIR, my friends and colleagues Jeff Cohen and Martin Lee were generous with insights and enthusiasm.

For Cheryl Higgins, my appreciation is enormous and ineffable.

Norman Solomon

THE INTREPID LINGUISTS LIBRARY

PEOPLE SAY THE DARNDEST THINGS...

"Sir Francis Drake circumcised the world with a 100-foot clipper."

"In 1957, Eugene O'Neil won a Pullet Surprise."

"Illiterate? Write today for free help."

Don't miss these side-splitting treasuries from The Intrepid Linguist's Library...

- ☐ **Anguished English** *Richard Lederer* 20352-X $5.95
- ☐ **It's Raining Cats and Dogs...and Other Beastly Expressions** *Christine Ammer* 20507-7 $5.95
- ☐ **Get Thee to a Punnery** *Richard Lederer* 20499-2 $5.95
- ☐ **Demonic Mnemonics** *Murray Suid* 20647-2 $5.95
- ☐ **The Superior Person's Book of Words** *Peter Bowler* 20407-0 $5.95
- ☐ **Remembrance of Things Fast** *Susan Ferraro* 20704-5 $5.95
- ☐ **The Devil's Dictionary** *Ambrose Bierce* 20853-X $5.99
- ☐ **The Diabolical Dictionary of Modern English** *R. W. Jackson* 20591-3 $5.95
- ☐ **Fighting Words** *Christine Ammer* 20666-9 $5.95
- ☐ **Gallimaufry To Go** *J. Bryan, III* 20775-4 $5.95
- ☐ **Spoonerisms, Sycophants and Sops** *Donald Chain Black* 20896-3 $5.95
- ☐ **The Phrases That Launched 1,000 Ships** *Nigel Rees* 20824-6 $5.99
- ☐ **Fumblerules** *William Safire* 21010-0 $5.99

At your local bookstore or use this handy page for ordering:

DELL READERS SERVICE, DEPT. DIL
2451 South Wolf Road, Des Plaines, IL 60018

Please send me the above title(s). I am enclosing $_____.
(Please add $2.50 per order to cover shipping and handling.) Send
check or money order—no cash or C.O.D.s please.

Ms./Mrs./Mr. _____

Address _____

City/State _____ Zip _____

DIL-6/92

Prices and availability subject to change without notice. Please allow four to six weeks for delivery.